Bluebonnets, Firewheels, and Brown-Eyed Susans:

or

Poems New and Used From the
Bandera Rag and Bone Shop

Selected Poetry by David Lee

Day's Work, 1990

Paragonah Canyon, 1990

My Town, 1995

Covenants (with William Kloefkorn), 1996

Wayburne Pig, 1997

The Fish, 1997

A Legacy of Shadow: Selected Poems, 1999

News from Down to the Café: New Poems, 1999

Incident at Thompson Slough, 2002

So Quietly the Earth, 2004

In a House Made of Time (with William Kloefkorn), 2010

Stone Wind Water, 2011

Texas Wild Flowers, 2011

Moments of Delicate Balance (with William Kloefkorn), 2011

Last Call, 2014

Bluebonnets, Firewheels, and Brown-Eyed Susans

or

Poems New and Used From the Bandera Rag and Bone Shop

David Lee

Utah Poet Laureate, 1997-2002

WingsPress

San Antonio, Texas
2017

Bluebonnets, Firewheels, and Brown-eyed Susans, or, Poems
New and Used From the Bandera Rag and Bone Shop
© 2017 by Wings Press, for David Lee

Cover painting © 2016 by Kimberly Harris

First Wings Press Edition

Paperback ISBN-13: 978-1-60940-520-5
Ebooks
ePub ISBN: 978-1-60940-521-2
Kindle/mobipocket ISBN: 978-1-60940-522-9
Library PDF ISBN: 978-1-60940-523-6

Wings Press
627 E. Guenther
San Antonio, Texas 78210
Phone/fax: (210) 271-7805
On-line catalogue and ordering:www.wingspress.com
All Wings Press titles are distributed to the trade by
Independent Publishers Group
www.ipgbook.com

Library of Congress Cataloging-in-Publication Data

Lee, David, 1944 August 13-
Uniform title: Poems. Selections
Title: Bluebonnets, fireweels, and brown-eyed susans, or,
Poems new and used from the Bandera Rag and Bone Shop /
David Lee
San Antonio, TX: Wings Press, 2017.
ISBN 978-1-60940-520-5 (pbk. : alk. paper); ISBN 978-1-
60940-521-2 (ePub ebook); ISBN 978-1-60940-522-9 (kin-
dle/mobipocket ebook); ISBN 978-1-60940-523-6 (library
pdf)
Subjects: (Topical): Rural women--Texas--Poetry,|
(Geographical): Texas--Poetry | Lee, David, 1944-
LC classification: PS3562.E338 B5 2017
Dewey classification: 811/.54

Contents

Bereshith: In the Beginning

I was, I believe, four when my beloved grandmother who, within the past hour, had told me I was, "her favorite little boy in the whole world," picked me up by the hair of my head and flung me into the corner of her living room in Matador, Texas and told me I must "stay there for an hour or all afternoon," expanding to the threshold of eternity, I suspect, until I learned my lesson once and for all and promised her and Godamitey-Himself that never again ever would the words, "I'm bored" ever issue forth from my lips and that I should "tell myself a joke or a story or whatever it takes to learn what He put between my ears as the greatest gift He could ever make," and I remember taking a subaltern deity's ransom value of time, at least up to eight seconds, searching the corner for worms I could eat and then die to show her how sorry she would be, and then turning to the problem of a joke or story, neither of which I had a goose's idea of how to create or tell except the remembrance of how Dandy and my uncles did it and how everyone laughed except the one it was about and so I created my first original story set in the church house and to make it a joke I added boogers, the funniest thing I knew, and I pulled one out over a foot long and turned around and stood up in my pew and showed it to Mrs. Hartman who hated my cockle spaniel named Honey and who I knew my grandmother didn't like because she was stiff necked and uncircumcised of heart and said it at the break-fast table and she screamed and fainted and fell out of her pew onto the floor and her snuff mop fell out of her sleeve where I knew she hid it and went clang-spang on the floor and the preacher said, "Oh precious baby Jesus," and grandmother went hee hee hee snort hee because that's how she laughed and I knew I'd said my first story out loud because when I turned around she was laughing and crying because as a member of the churchofchrist she knew laughter was a potential sin perhaps even as evil as dancing and told me I could come out of the corner now if I promised to never say that word again and I promised and crossed my heart to make it true but I told her I wanted to make up another story so I'd come out later and I did and got to tell it at the supper table and I've kept that promise for almost seventy years, and that's pretty much how it happened once upon a time, and this book is for my grandmother, with love. And your grandmother, too.

This book was inspired by women from small town
West Texas, 1948-1962 who, for better or worse,
molded me into the person I ultimately became.
In that light, this book is lovingly made as
my remembrance to you, yall, all yall.

Bluebonnets, Firewheels, and Brown-Eyed Susans

or

Poems New and Used From the Bandera Rag and Bone Shop

Slow Waking of Morning from Dream

The true meaning of eternity is Today.
—Philo

Crows stare
and mutter in foreign tongues
as they line the branches
of a dying live oak,
gargoyles on twilight's ramparts

A white daylight armadillo's tail moon
hangs like a closing parenthesis
south of Polly's Peak
where sun's fingers grasp,
pull the earth down from darkness

Day crawls into bloodshot sky
like an incoming mirage,
spreads a scarlet foam
across the shoulder dunes
of hill country horizon

A sand hill crane hen
perched on one leg
in a wildflower meadow sixty years past—
a feathered memory in dreammist,
head tucked beneath its wing

Veal, 1948

All afternoon grandmother
dressed the meat
divided the cuts
steaks and chops
a small roast
for the ice box
and sliced the round
into thin pieces which
for the first time
she didn't pound
with a saucer's edge

and for the meal
a private portion
chicken fried
for everyone at the table
including kids
so tender adults weren't required
to do cutting
the savor of fresh beef
filling the air
on the tongue
lingering in the mind

"This is so good"
"So so good, mama"
"Never so tender"
"Where'd you get this meat?"
and grandmother

head down to her plate
as if in prayer
"Milk cow shed her calf"
"Shed her calf?"
"Still born"

A Hymn for Pearl

A day none of us who were there
will ever forget was when
they buried Pearl Nance
who wanted more than any woman
who ever lived not to be one

from her twelfth birthday
she was God's experiment in gravity
any part you would have thought
could stick out got too big
pointed straight down
even her neck was a broken swivel
where her head studied only sidewalk

wore men's britches and boots
snap-up front shirts with W.B. Garrett brown
and fingernailfile snuffmop in the pockets
she could hork and spit and curse and lean
into a pickup fender
never did get the rhythm
to make it seem recreational
no one faulted her
for not making the effort

it was on a Thursday of a week
that hadn't seemed heretofore memorable
she went behind the cafe counter
late for evening coffee with this pint
she brought down from Johnston still
poured half a filled cup brimful

said Here Brother Coy
let me buy you coffee this one time
him sitting in his booth alone
like the cormorant in the tree
in the garden of life
with a harpoon to shove into any words
he heard and thought fit to drag up
for one of his sermons he brooded on
as a responsible affliction for the Lord
to visit on each and all of his many enemies
he and the Lord shared
in their enthusiasm for the gospel

the only thing he could think of to say was
Why thank you ma'am
we struck as dumb as Zacharias
our meditation on the wish for his death
interrupted for the moment
and then Why this here coffee has some bite to it
and then Is it any possibility of a refill?
to which

Pearl said Let me bring you
a fresh cup Brother Coy
and then a third
and lo
he who we knew as so filled with hate
he'd rot fast when he died
so E.U. the cemetery tender always had a hole
dug and ready for ahead of time just in case
began to smile
began he to even laugh
for the first time we knew of ever

no one there could have predicted
the Lord's hand would reach out
and touch that one
it was a terrible mystery to us all
but when he stood and embraced Pearl
with a Christian's brotherly kiss
when she brought the fourth
it was a lesson
to never underestimate the power of the Lord
or the goodness of fine whiskey

and then she said
Brother Coy I am become singful
and he said Let us make a joyful noise
before the Lord
and began a spate of hymns
that tested the endurance of all the gods

fourteen times B.L. Wayburn had to unlock
the cafe door so half the town
and all the regulars could come in
until four in the morning from page one
"Trust and Obey" of Christian Hymnal #2
to "How Great Thou Art" pasted on the backside cover
memorized by heart in four-part harmony
plus two others unknown to music
so R.B. and Ollie could join in
all together singing flatout

even old blind George Albany came in
the front door for once with his pencil and chewing gum tray
and perfect-pitch tenor we never knew of
did the solo in "Lead Shining Light"
Pearl rising to the occasion with her obligato
"Out of the Ivory Palace" Coy bawled on

and admitted for the first time
she thought in a previous life
maybe she'd been one of those eunuchs
in that Viennie boy's choir
and how much she must have loved it
as something to look forward to

Coy leading "I Come to the Garden Alone"
from the top of the counter
in between every stanza saying One more time
to tell the Lord you really mean it
so hot in that cafe by then
Baby Jesus was wilting off the inside front cover
of the hymnals in their racks
in their pews in their respective churchhouses
scattered across the dark streets of our town
joined together for the first time in song
the only time any of us who knew him
professed any love for that sad man
and then she died

took three days to decide
she'd never been inside a churchhouse once
since she was old enough to choose
it wouldn't be right to inflict
the ceremony on her then
we all came to the graveyard instead

So many people they had to stand on chairs
and almost all the preachers including Brother Coy
to see and hear B.L. Wayburn speak the words
we all said as testimony
over coffee he wrote down
how when he came to the part
She was the founder of the Thursday Night Choir

which only met that one time
it must have been the inspiration of the Lord
us all breaking out together at once
with "Just As I Am" flatout

every one of us who knew
could see with our eyes closed
her big chest swell up
knowing she was no longer alone
until all those pearl snaps on her cowboy shirt
popped open one by one

The First Time Kristine Thornton Spoke During Town Board Meeting

addressee of comment unacknowledged

Your life is so dull
standing beside the pavement
is a adventure

*From sidebar minutes of the
monthly Town Board Meeting,
October 1948*

Lilly McCree Snaps a Pistachio Shell with Her Fingernails While Staring Out the High School Library Window On the Opening Day of Fall Term

Over the Mojave Desert
a year ago
a jet crashed
the sound barrier
and the world stood in silence

Today the radiance
of a lonely contrail
frames a corner of sky,
the lingering pop echo
spiraling in the mind's ear

Evening Solemnities and Recapitulations

Invocation

Bus Pennell said to Arvin Elithorpe
at the Dew Drop Inn
Hey Arvilbald
I heard it was a real hullerbaloo
at the political meeting this afternoon
Arvin said That would be a fact
Bus said You gone tell us about it
from memory or do we all
have to buy you a cold refresher first?

Recollection

Arvin said It wouldn't of been nothing special
except it was a foreign out of state Senator
they brought in who wants
to be a Supreme Court Judge someday
to make a speech on proper obstruction methodology
for anyone being a dues paying member
of the true American political Great Option Party
Cleon Thuett said That sounds
like something we could hear at a church house
if somebody had a mind to go listen
Arvin said Yep that would also be a fact
Wallace Jennings said Was that the rodeo gunfight?
Arvin said No that happened after
the speech when it was question and answer
LaVerne Sims stood up and said
Senator Suptions I have a question for you
he looked at her and said Why LaVerne Evans

can I even think that's you?
she said Yes Jeb it is I, now LaVerne Sims
he said I don't believe I've lain eyes on you
in a coon and a half's age
she said That would be about right Jeb
but my question is a bit on the personal side
he said Well LaVerne my old lady friend I truly think
we're all party members and believers here
you just fire away and I'll do my best
to give you the answer you want to hear
she said Jeb I've heard a true story
confirmed rumor that you and Raelynn
got yourselves a Mexican divorce

Senator Suptions went frog-eyed and blanch-faced
said We thought no I thought anyway
it wouldn't come out quite so quick
how was it you come to hear LaVerne
it wasn't Mexican I got it at Las Vegas, Nevada?
she said I suspect you know
all about the kinfolk family news pipe stream
that doesn't stop at the stateline border
weren't yall married somewhere upward
of a good forty years? the Senator said
LaVerne I believe you already know
that to be the fact of the matter
she said And didn't yall have
four children from that relationship?
he said You already know that's true LaVerne
it's no sense trying to embarrass me on it

she said Well Senator Jeb Suptions my old gentleman friend
what I want to know as my question to you
is now that you're got yourself a genuine
bona fide Las Vegas, Nevada divorce and your marriage

of forty years upward is dispensed of
to Raeyln what about those children
now mostly full grown and scattered
all over the known world of our United States
extending even beyond the borders of Texas
will they still be brothers and sisters
or will they revert back
to first cousins once removed?
and then she set down

Benediction

What was it the part about Judge Parker?
said Cleotis Ledbitter
Arvin Elithorpe said That happened outside
after they call the rally to a quickstop halt
told us to go on home now and contribute money
to elections of party members at the appointed season
he asked LaVerne how she come
to think up such a pregnant question
for the esteemed Senator
wanting to be a Supreme Court Judge someday
she said Oh it was something I recalled
from my youthful time we learned
in fifth grade I think from the State Weekly Reader
our teacher called a Thought Problem
I remembered and brought it up to mind
then I recited it from the heart
I knew he couldn't answer it back then
I wanted to see if he could do any better now
when he could see the practicality of education
but he doesn't seem to have matured a bit
and gentlemen that's all she had to say
and that's exactly all they were to it

Memoir: Dawn After the Great Sandstorm,
July 1949:
Morning Chores and Egg Gathering

Hot inside the barn
caprock a bent shimmer
of omnipotent deception
the devil's water spread
over sand dunes
dead wind already broiled
by the sheet iron roof

prairie threeawn tufts
outside the door
prostrate
neck deep in drift
deathbed protestants
without a mirror
in the dying room
praying to gods
they never before
envisioned

smell of barnyard
in the scoured air
as if the galoshed whirlwind
traipsed through a feed yard
and came home
in work clothes

earth heaving
against the pale sky

like the chest
of the barren
Spotted Poland China sow
sleeping her black
and white dreams
premonitions
of the world
awaiting

Conversation Between LaVeda Latham
and the John Deere Calendar in the Kitchen Overheard
by her Daughter Cara Sue

I wish the Good Lord
would try and believe in rain
as hard as I try
to believe in Him

On a Short Early Winter Walk
(when I meant to think
about perching buzzards)

a little immigrating southwind
clutched my leg like a tendril,
the rushing leaves around and about
moving toward their hidden nests

when I said Hola nieta
she said Buenas dias, abuela
such a fine day to be out,
let us finish this walk together

Summer Drought Idyll:
City Park Restroom (found poem)

Monday

    Shithouse close do to water shortege

Wednesday

    Men side out house close do to water shortege

Friday

    Men side close
    do to water shortege

    Wemen side Open
    plese try to cut it off short

Saturday

    Men Side Close
    do to water shortege

    Wemen Side Open
    plese try to cut it off short
    When possibal

Also Any one have extraie catalogs
would be subject to thanks
is needed soon as possibal on wemen side

Sunday

Pray for Rain
if you go to church
if you don't do
we need it all the help we can get
when its free try

Shithouse still close
do to water shortege
caint hep it no fuckin water

One Reason Why You Didn't Want Kristine Thornton To Talk During Town Board Meeting

While Arguing Over Redistricting With Joe Bob Trammel

If the Lord wanted you
to have an empty head
and a cob up your ass
He'd of put popcorn seeds
in your daddy's spurem

*From sidebar minutes of the
monthly Town Board Meetings
19 September 1950*

Gethsemane
Caprock Supplications in the Cathedral of Wind

The tomato plant
long dead
buried
and unburied
and then buried again
by the wind
as if it did it
to check and see
if it might be still alive
or not

⊷·⊶✦⊷·⊶

LaVeda squatting in the sand
head down
What you doing? said Suetta
Thinking
About what?
Dunno
just got started
Spect you'll get to rain before long
Probley so

⊷·⊶✦⊷·⊶

wind wobbling
like a wonkey wheel
on a grocery cart
a lake apparition

over the caprock
Hell's soul
turning itself inside out
mimics the mist
that even the widow's mite
can't coax

cowled
in a blanket
of wind

Still thinking?
No
believe I might be praying now
For rain?
Yep
Working?
Not so far
don't see any clouds
Looks all dry
from here on
Seems like it
Give it some time
something might break

---

cloudy
the only star burned
down to the last option
an agnostic's votive
barely flickering

whispered suppliance
to the wind
Lord of the Dance
fire in one talon
rain in the other

night
black as the inside
of a baby's casket
lined with pages
from the Book of Revelation

You smell rain?
Not yet
that's the scent of moonlight
behind that cloud
wrapping itself up
in wind
trying to work through

You think any of this
is doing any good?
You got any
better ideas?

splightlight

sky closed with a darkness

that hammered like Jael's tentpeg
through night's eardrum
then a rumble
wind shudder

as if an earthquake
passed through the sky's yard
dragging fever behind
like a leashed shoat

⸻

wind exhausted

darkened moon
La Llorena wandering
with a spent candle
in a nightjar

so quiet
an owl's heartbeat
a bull drum
inside its folded wings

⸻

Could bring down a tornader

Long as it's a wet one I'll take it

Even then?

Even then

You staying out in it?

Yep.

Albert might say
If it comes
you could get rained on
like a sonofabitch

Then you tell Albert
I'll be wet
like a sonofabitch
A happy sonofabitch

Okay Lord
it's set up
I've done my part

get to work
throw us a cloudburst
that rips holes in the sky

do that
and I will forgive You
everything

I promise You
that

Leatrice Justice Bids the Missionaries Adieu

You young Truechurch Elders
spoke a right finely polished speech
and requited yourselves nicely
but I need to tell you from the bottom

your ideas of heaven wouldn't hold me
for two days much less
time and all eternity
and from the middle

your bodacious list of all I mustn't do
to live a righteous The Church approved life
encompasses nearly every single item
I enjoy at this fork in the graveled road

I chose as my path of following
and from the top I need to say
I have no fear of any perpetually angry god
holding a One True Way last judgment

and that if I have a choice I'll vote no
and skip the whole afterlife affair
but what does worry me
more than a widow's smidgen

is the concern I wake up dead
and find out doing the Hokey Pokey
really is what it's all about
and I wasted my entire pathetic life

not participating in enough of it
which places us exactly at the much ado bifurcation
of here we are and there you go all for nothing
and that pretty much is what I have to offer

unless you two boys in your Sunday
go-to-meeting clothes would care for another slice
of my true family unshared recipe brandy apple
beer battered crust pie before you go

Aftermath

a found poem

How much
you think we got? said Suetta
Got a pint here said LaVeda
A pint?
Yep
How's that?
I put a quart Mason jar
on the porch
it's half full

Coy

Mark 1:17

Reverend Coy Stribling told his mama
he was just real discouraged
couldn't get the attendance
or the collection plate
at the Church of God of Prophecy of
Holy and Divine Revelation up one bit
it was flatlined almost a year
he didn't know what to do

she said If you're gone be
one of Jesuses' fishers for men
you got to find you some good bait
and that's what they are to it
put your whole mind on that

his wife said Poor Coy he thought hard
with sweatstains down to his shirt cuffs
turning brown almost for a week
she had to put bluing in the warsher
to lighten it up
read the scriptures
till his lips was so sore
he couldn't barely even talk
then like a thunder of lightning
run over to the telephone book
looked up a number to call
that would be the answer
for all his problems

got Ella Mae Blodgett on the line
by that afternoon made her the offer
three dollars a week to come to Sunday School
then church service at eleven
wearing that snow cone pointed brassiere
under her pullover black sweater
the tight one with the gold leaf
draping right acrost
where her heart would be
if it was on the outside
Ella Mae said that was more
than she made babysitting of a night
she'd give it a try

had her sit up front
second row back and one
of the Sisters who cleaned at Judy's
got her a Gideon bible out of a motel room
to hold in her lap
a red one

by third week Sunday School
almost doubled and most
stayed for church
crowded up to the front
so popular Coy's wife said
if he'd get a chiropractor license
to unstraighten crick necks
on Sunday afternoon
he'd be a rich man by Christmas
but it was a personal tragedy instead
collection plate didn't go up
most visitors were high school students
only there to check it out
without tithing admission

then Ella Mae told him
she'd need a raise to keep it up
didn't mind Sunday School
but she'd need another dollar
to stay through the sermon
Coy said I can appreciate that but
she said No you caint
you don't have to listen
that's worth proper wages
which he flat didn't have

so the fishing expedition
came up with an empty stringer
except Ella Mae got asked out
for four different dates
by three Christian boys
one of which she ended up
wearing his FFA pin prominent
on the gold leaf of her black sweater
right where it draped over her heart
Coy wished her good luck
promised he would make up and say
a apostolic prayer just for her
and if it worked out he would preach
the nuptial ceremony for free

Ella Mae told him He couldn't never know
just how much she appreciated his offer
and that she'd give half of it back
if he'd promise to cut his part
of the wedding sermon by the same amount
and Reverend Coy told Ella Mae
she had her a deal

To a Poor Old Woman (In the Rest Home)

after William Carlos Williams

Sal si puedes.

Sal si
Puedes.

Sal
si puedes,
Abuelita.

Andale.

Neighbors

Cigarettes, whiskey and wild, wild women
—Red Ingalls

Bullards and the Bloodworths lived
down the street from each other both ways
had about nine kids more or less
nobody ever got a good count
on the Bloodworths so it could have been more
like a whole backyard full of hens
and ducks chasing grasshoppers
it was always bloody nose, skinned knee
I'm gone tell my mama she'll whup your ast
even after the sun went down
you could hear *Fibber McGee* four blocks away
everybody had it cranked up so loud
to drown them out in the whole neighborhood
especially when they ever got on the churchhouse

they'd line up across the street from each other
and take turns hollering
    My mama said yall aint going to heaven when you died
    Well my mama says onliest ones there are the Baptists
    My mama said Jesustchrist he never heard of no
        Baptist Church
    Well he goddam never went to no Pennycosted
        Not one without no flags especially
    My mama said them is idolarties and you're a sonofabitch
    My mama says your mama is full of shit

then they'd throw rocks
until one or the other would call them
in for suppertime

one July when it was hot
Billy Joe Bullard ran home
told his mama Rosemary Bloodworth
said her mama told her
he couldn't never be no sunbeam for Jesust
Missus Bullard had had it
took off her apron
threw it on the floor
slammed the screen door when she left
went down the street
so mad you could hear her feet in the gravel
hollered Lucille Bloodworth out of her house
said What did you say to that one girl about my Billy Joe?
it was just as hot in Lucille Bloodworth's house that day
she said I never said one thing about that boy of yours
you keep him at home if you don't want him in my yard
is he the one that has dogshit on his shoes?
Missus Bullard said Did you say
Christjesust never wanted my boy?
We don't have no dog
Lucille Bloodworth said That boy never
been truly warshed in the blood of the lamb

that did it
Missus Bullard swung on her like a cement mixer
next thing they were both spitting, slapping and clawing
then they grabbed hair
street looked like four of Bus Pennel's hounds
slunk down it looking for a place to lie down
and die of mange in the crawl space under somebody's back porch
hair and blood and snot all over
both of them screaming razorblades
just like two hogs fighting over a lace tablecloth
all the kids hollering and bellering

this one boy of theirs was being an Indian
with a bow and arrow nine years old named Jimmy Paul James
took and licked the stopper and shot
hit Missus Bullard and the arrow stuck
on the bottom of her arm where it hung down
she being a fleshy woman
every time she'd give Lucille Bloodworth's hair a pull
the arrow would jump up and down
kids commenced yelling like sheet iron
    Shoot her again
    Don't shoot my mama
    Let me shoot it
    Shoot her on the floppers
her shirt torn open on the front
until this one little girl three years old named Wanda Ann Bullard
got right in between them, looked up
said Mama Jimmy Paul James done shot your with a error

the women let go of each other and stood right up
Lucille Bloodworth reached out, grabbed that arrow and jerked
    it off
you could hear the rubberstopper pop all the way down the street
broke it in half
Missus Bullard hollered Oh my Lard I'm gone have a bruice big
    as a piepan
Lucille Bloodworth said Goddam ever ONE of you, who done that?
all those kids quit yelling right then
with their mouths hanging open

if he'd just stood there nobody would have ever known
neither one of the women could have told
which kids were theirs or the other's
but Jimmy Paul James got coweyed
threw his arrows straight up in the air
he would have strangled his bow to death

and it would have been deafened for life from the scream
if it had been alive when he took off
for about nine steps
broke the string when he threw it down so hard on the road
it sounded like the entire Seventh Calvary
chasing one Indian after Custer
the way they took after him down the blocks to his house
he ran inside and locked the screen door
shut the woodendoor
went around and pulled all the windowshades down
got in bed with a pillow over his head
they banged on the door and hollered
kids chunked clods at the house for an hour
only broke one window
but nobody was home that day
his mama and daddy worked for a living
said they'd call sonofabitching Sheriff Red Floyd by god
they'd have him arrested and thrown in jail
with the murderers and the bootleggers
they'd put one of Charley Baker's idiots in there with him
and tell it he had candy in his pockets
none of it did any good

they waited in the sun for him to come out
and finally when he didn't
they all went home
Lucille Bloodworth said You keep your kids away from my chirren
Missus Bullard said I don't care if I don't never see you again
she said That's two days before I'll lain eyes on you
said You go to hell you white trash
said So I can hear you hollering for ice water
all the way down the street
all the kids went in their houses and it was quiet that night
for once

three days later
all the Bloodworth kids lined up by the Bullard's car
their faces washed and a clean shirt
Jimmy Paul James shoved in between
to go to vacation Bible school
when Missus Bullard was cramming them in
one said My mama told us we don't have to come back
till we had all the sandwich and soda pop we wanted for dinner
so don't let you be in a hurry
Moses couldn't have made a dent in those kids to see
out the back window through the carmirror
like the Omaha hogtrain to Los Angeles
arms and legs hanging out the windows
wallowing each other like a Prince Albert can of night crawlers
you could hear them half a mile off
singing
    red and yellar, black and white
    we love Jesust just for spite
    all the little chirren of the world

Old Man Cummings' Story
He Told His Neighbor Malouf's Son That Summer
About a Month Before He Died

It was this one summer back then
I's young about the time most kids
getting out of school but I'd done quit
old man Cummings had me helping him
lifting all this heavy weight on a wagon load
we made a tote and sat in the shade to rest
he must have started remembering
commenced talking, said

summer clover jingle jangle

he'd taken and put his hand in his pocket
pulled out this silver dollar
looked at it like he'd never seen it before
all smooth so you couldn't even tell
the man on the side, picture and all the words
rubbed off from being carried so long
it was meadow clover stretching out
green and yellow all over
I didn't say anything, he talked, said
I was seventeen they come in wagons
putting on Gypsy carnivals
everybody in town wanted them to go on
knew they'd steal whatall's loose and laying around
we all went to the tent that night anyway
they paid me a dollar to water horses
I worked all afternoon hard at seventeen for a dollar

She had eyes that laughed
same color as them fancy shoes
laugh like silver bobbles
on a red and blue velvet dress
color of midnight
even in the dark I seen me
looking back from those black eyes
I wasn't scared
she shown me slow, easy
the whole field of green and yellow clover
bells on her shoes real soft
jingle jangle

So many nights I can't sleep
smell comes in the window after me
when my wife's alive times I lain the whole night
beside her shaking, awake, all that dark
tearing holes in me
nothing I could do but stay there
listening for the sound of silver windbells
kids in the next room, sleeping,
nobody could see it or hear it but me
summer clover jingle jangle

he sat there staring at that money in his hand
almost like he's talking to it
like he'd done forgotten I was there, too
but he didn't say anything more
put it in his pocket and closed his eyes
I could tell he's smelling the summer grass
the storytelling to me all over for then
but when I close my eyes and think about it even now
I can hear the sound I heard way back when
of some silver bells jinglejangling in the wind

Where I'm From

Where I'm from you served the overstayed preacher boiled
  okra
And sat him in a chair by a table post so he couldn't cross
  his legs

Where I'm from somebody at the breakfast table always
  wanted a half fried still alive
sunny side up egg and poured ketchup on, beat up the yolk
  and ate it with a spoon

Where I'm from at church parties they always brought baked
  ham
With pineapple slices atop the kids weren't allowed to eat

Where I'm from the old people poured their coffee into
  saucers and slurped
And the kids were told slurping their food is goddam bad
  manners

Where I'm from saying goddam out loud in public was never
  done
except by those who do, and more than admit they say, do

Feat on a Crisp Autumn Wednesday

Out on the feather run
leaf gold like silken horses
trots through the thousand eyed camouflage
of November's immaculate red and brown laughter

One Reason Why You Didn't Want Kristine Thornton To Talk During Town Board Meetings

on an unnamed citizen
running for town board

He's meteoaker
just trash not worth picking up;
a bucket with two holes
in the bottom
and a tore out pouring edge

From sidebar minutes of the monthly
Town Board Meetings
12 May 1953

T. L. Jones Icehouse Feed and Seed
All Your Agricultural Needs
A Christmas Triptych

after S. T. Coleridge's "Christabel"

Part One

Hottest day of the summer
Adam Graben drove in to town
went straight up to T. L. Jones
in the feedstore
said Mr. T. L. I need help with my new bull
T. L. Jones said What kind of help
do you need Mr. Adam Graben?
Adam Graben said He aint proving up
doesn't seem to be working the herd
all he wants to do is graze
and stand in the tree shade
all them cows staring at him
wondering what he thinks
he's out there for

T. L. Jones said I don't know
for sure what to tell you
but I just got a new product
out on the unproven market
I can sell you to speculate on

went to his storeroom
came back with a box of pills
like they'd choke a rhinoceros
said This is them
I don't have no idea

how good they might or not work
What do I do? said Adam Graben

That will be the hard part
said T. L. Jones
You have to figger a way
to get that new bull to swaller these

I think if he was my bull
I'd put him in a squeeze chute
you can close up on him
force feed one at a time
ever day for awhile
see if it'll work

you have to get the pill
on the back of his tongue
so he'll take it down or choke
yougn use a bolus stick
or a long handled wooden spoon
for the big poke

might just work
I was you I'd give it a try
they don't cost too much yet
to not be worth the effort
and I'll give you a good buy

Part Two

Coldest day of the year so far
Adam Graben drove in to town
on a Thursday
went straight up to T. L. Jones
in the feedstore with the stove crunk up high

all the farmers inside
like a murder of crows
reminding each other
how it had been
and whatall it meant
on a day as far as they could tell
about as cold as a shithouse in hell

T. L. Jones said Mr. Adam Graben come tell us
what you giving Miss Lilith for Christmas
sit down by the stove
stay awhile with your feet up
and take off your hat

Adam Graben said Mr. T. L.
I need your help again
with my new red bull
you done me good with last summer
you remember that

T. L. Jones said Not exactly
you need to refreshen me
which air new red bull
Adam Graben said Oh yes you do
he was standing in the tree shade
not working the heifers
like he was posta do

you give me some huge bull pills
to get his mind off grass and
get it behind his tongue
to get his pecker up
like a long handled wooden spoon
him out of the barn
out there in the field on the ball

T. L. Jones said I did that all
by myself without these gentlemen's advice?
Adam Graben said Yessir you did
charged me fifteen dollars
for a box of it
and I need some more
right now today

I just don't seem to remember said T. L. Jones
it must have been too long ago
you gone have to help me think
what kind of pill it was

They was big ones said Adam Graben
about the size of the bottom joint
on your working thumb
more or less light blue
with white speckles
all the way through

kindly tasties
just a little bit
like a striped cane
of Christmas peppermint

Part Three

Christmas Eve on a Tuesday that year
Lilith Graben got the pickup
drove in to town
Right through a red light
according to Deputy Sheriff Junior Shepherd
who followed her to T. L. Jones
Icehouse Feed and Seed
where she stopped the Graben truck

turned off the key
got out and walked
right in the slamming front door

Deputy Sheriff Junior Shepherd said
By the time I could foller
she was standing like Baby Jesus in the Temple
amongst the farmers
bellied up to the stove in their cheers

said Mr. T. L. Jones
I have something to say to you
T. L. Jones said Well Miss Graben
what's Sandy Claus abringing
you and Mr. Adam for Christmas?

Lilith Graben said Mr. T. L.
I didn't come here today
to have no conversation
or to talk about what we are or not
getting or keeping for Christmas

I came here to tell you a thing if I could
and I want you to listen to me real good

Lilith Graben said Mr. T. L.
don't you never ever
for any or no reason whatsothehellever
sell my husband any of your Peter-up pills again
I don't care if it's for his bull
or a horse or a hog or a chicken or a dog
you don't do it in any size
or shape or color or taste
I mean no more again ever period
not for any reason, case or sake

and if you do
I mean to tell you right here
right now I will come back
like Christ's resurrection
carrying the first hammer I can
lay my hands upon to this store
whatever day of the week it comes on

I will hit you with that hammer
and try to knock you through that wall
just as hard as I can
right in your balls

and I swear to you
that is exactly precisely what I will do
then without another word
she turned and walked across that wooden floor
with the rattling sound of the doorpane slam
she disappeared through the feedstore door
then all became as quiet as falling snow
not a sound anywhere inside that store any more

Coda Finis

in bed beside his second wife
later on that Christmas night
Deputy Sheriff Junior Shepherd remembered
he forgot to write Miss Lilith her ticket
for running that red light

but after thinking it over
he came to believe without remorse or spite
in a hundred years no one would ever know
and that was just gone have to be all right

it was time for forgiveness to everbody
for Merry Christmas and good night

Housedogs

Ollie McDougald when I sat down
at the counter to have coffee said
he didn't want to talk about it
I saw he's down in the mouth and said Whar?
he said It aint nothing to speak of
I let it go and watched
while he stirred his coffee without any sugar
or milk in it with his spoon studying
said finally If it's any of your business
it's that goddam fycet
my brother-in-law by marriage taken
and given to my wife she name Sweetie
now that sonofabitch lives in the house
all day and at night in our bed
it's about ruirnt my whole life
marriage done shot to hell
and dogshit all over the yard
what am I posta do?
B.L. Wayburn running coffee and cash register
listening in said It aint nothing
about all this I don't know
so if you curious you just axe me

I been married three times and had nine dogs
two of them in the house by two wormen
I'll tell you now free of charge
two things you can set your watch to

and live a life by if you want
First is a married womern can only love a thing
if she can pity it and then run over it
which is why they let them things
sit in their laps smelling them
watching t.v. in the house
whenever they scratch on the door to get in
And the second is what your daddy
should of told you in high school that
a womern's love is like morningdew
sparkles like a diamond in a goat's ass
it might land on a red garden rose or a turd
it won't know the difference
you better make yourself accustom
she ever has to choose between you
and that shiteater you just as well
get on down the gravelway kicking road apples
one of them might be dew wet
remember it caint necessarily help it
her and it just likes the shine
so all you can do is scrape off your shoes
come on in and sit down
try to outlive it and not get anothern
that dog's as permanent and official
as Judge Parker in his courthouse
you want to stay married
make you a compromise and do it her way
That's all they are to it

What my Grandmother Told Me
Her Grandmother Told Her

General Sherman said, I apologize, ma'am,
But I bring Hell temporarily
To force this war to a close and by doing so
I may save yours and others' sons' lives.

And she said, General,
You follow duty and do what you must.
Last night I watched the place I call home
Burn like the Devil's Hell had invaded

And today I find you charming,
A man I could have loved
In another life,
Another world.

Because I cannot love you
in this life,
My wish is that we may spend
Eternity together, in Hell

And that I will dance in flames
As I watch you and everything
You were reared to know and love
Burn for ever and a day.

And she said the General
Saluted her and as he turned his horse
Said, Ma'am, I fear
Your wish will be my command.

And Another Reason

directed to Mayor Topham
after a lengthy dissertation

If you were my husband
I'd get a turn-off switch
welded onto my navel
so I could stay asleep
after you came home
and got in bed at night

*from sidebar minutes of the monthly
Town Board Meetings
14 June 1955*

Song E.U. Washburn, the Gravetender,
Heard Sung Between the Malouf and Cummings Plots
On a Saturday Evening

many a thought shall die which was not born of dream
— e. e. cummings

I remember a red covered bridge
and a yellow and black butterfly,
evening and a nighthawk
over moving water.
Her silver words turning the world
called the moon
like a great stone pulled up
from the earth and broken away,
its taproot sliding back soft
into the hill country's belly
while that white child
wandered like the lost thing I became
alone in the twilight sky.

I put a buckle
on that moon and the jinglejangle sound
of her voice hanging in the air,
held it like a shiny dollar in my hand
one with the night
until a cloud covered me
and the moon climbed into dream,
words swallowing us
like a gush of Rio Frio water.
When we had been
all was unchanged where we had gone:
moonlight, bridge, dust motes,
butterfly, silver river, the nightjar's song.

Conversation Overheard from a Back Booth on a Tuesday Afternoon After a Weekend Storm

1

That man sitting beside you
last night at the party
what a nice man he was.

Oh, Mama. Mama that man
he loves me. I think a lot.

Yes baby girl. Surely
I did know that.

2

when I was a girlchild
once and I was
when Daddy worked in the mine
he brought all his possibles
and responsibilities home on the porch
for us not to touch on a weekend
that the Lord made for pure pleasure

it was on a Friday passing
into Saturday morning
after him being away all week a miner
making dreamplay in their room
all that house breathing love
and a whole live grown-up man
walking in a part of my mind
I didn't think my mama

knew about either
in the night

I had to go out on the porch
alone with him in the midnight
with a giant storm throbbing
all around and inside
so I had to sit down
on Daddy's box from the mine
I didn't find out until tomorrow
was dynamites for the blasting

it was a wonderful
terrible storm that summer night
whole sky and house filled
with fire and thunder from all the gods
my body drenched with rain and sweat
until my nightgown held on to me
like love itself

I sat alone
with the shadows after the storm walked on
breathing in all the rainwallowed hay
and the yard and Mama's roses
opened and shed across the garden
glistening in the dreamlight
the whole live world exploded
and brought back together
by what happens
to us all, baby girl,
in the storm on a summer night

Preacher

In 1956 the First Baptists got a new preacher
The Right Reverend Pastor Brother Strayhan until
at a later date he earned a permanent alternate moniker
from the Southern Tennessee Ministerial Seminary
who toted an eight pound Bible claimed to have been given
upon graduation carrying a spinal straining approximately
forty ribbons marking citation pagination
all the imaginable colors of Joseph's patriarchal coat
that got him thrown into a holding tank pending reassignment
so that after he had shepherded them for a year's span
he took it upon himself to sporadically remind the flock
of his significance having received each ribbon
as a mark of his acknowledgement being designated
Outstanding in His Field as he worked himself
into an archetypal lather uplifting the ribbons
in his proverbial peroration toward Giving of the Invitation
swinging the tome like a veritable Chinese New Year's kite
above the podium in his exuberant desire for manifestation
so that Miss Vera Mae Bouchier the venerable Baptist
Matriarch after services on an extraordinarily warm spring
12:36 p.m. proclaimed she wished he would go
out and stand in his field some more
she had had a belly full of him and no dinner yet already

In particular he loved to preach on his calling by the Lord
to be his Servant when he was only sixteen years of age
met his lovely wife that same summer to the glory of God
Miss Bouchier said almost out loud she allowed that possiblity
all boys that age get called, some even on the telephone
but she had a premonition the Good Lord may well have

got an unlisted number that time, we all get it wrong
now and then that poor woman had a veritable passel of kids
all the Lord's will the oldest Debby Reynolds Strayhan
not even twelve Deacon James Lee Bowen
heard to whisper during communion She resembles
a inner tube without about half its air
why he's sure him and his Missus heard her two aisles over
in Piggly Wiggly once her feet drug so
wore out and it wasn't no way they could count her
to be even thirty and still known it was her
before they even seen her by the slouching sound

Even though he received his ministerial salary, parsonage
automobile and full electricity and water coverage
he remained convinced that in light of his sizeable family
it wasn't enough to get by on so that seemingly
every third Sunday the sermon concerned
the collection plate and the bread on the water
exercising in addition his prerogative to traverse
the township inquiring of all businesses
a ministerial discount and when denied stalking out
in an emblematic huff with the covert threat of calling
for a Christian boycott by all true believers in his faith
his children receiving half price discounts at the Garza Theatre
for Saturday matinee Roy Rogers extravaganzas
free meals at the school lunchroom
and complimentary family admission
to all Antelope Sporting, Cultural and Musical events

And so it came to pass that on a Thursday of a previously
non-memorable out-of-football-season month
the Strayhan clan sojourned to Miss Lela's Dew Drop Inn
for supper and stood in abeyance before the counter

awaiting Miss Lela's acknowledgement upon which
the Reverend gave parochial noddance to his eldest son
Billy Graham Strayhan to proceed with invocation
upon which the future missionary to the starving Ethopian
innocents opined How much is your menstral discount to eat here
my daddy says we need at least twenty percent?
Miss Lela being not a Baptist but a Presbyter
said Whar? whereupon the Right Reverend
in perfect clarification rejoined My family and I
receive discounts on the account of my being
a Minister of God of up to one half at most places
of business in this community and Deacon Eulis Robinson
one of the diners that evening rejoined in Christian piety
because he had no alternative Yes ma'am that's a fact
all the restaurant entourage rapt and sitting at full attention
enjoined to see if there might occur on this evening in Texas
a repetition of Moses'Exodus and the subsequent
parting of the north fork of the dry Brazos river
Miss Lela said con grande autorita Set down
I'll do my twenty percent one time

Benevolently waving away the intrusion of menu
God's Chosen ordered tunafish sandwiches
and a large glass of water with a lemon slice for his children
fried chicken for his lovely wife that being always
in perfect Christian conservatism the most for the money
and told the waitress Bring me a steak to eat tonight
my daughter in Christ
How would you like that steak cooked, then? she said
to which he rejoined Scriptural
whereupon she replied What? he said
Well done my good and faithful servant
leaned back in his chair and smiled
generously to the adulating audience

Miss Lela heard it beginning to end top to bottom
and in a voice purloined from Job's whirlwind
shouted across the wavering cafe
from the cash register to the cook
all in attendance harkened once again to attention
Fix that preacher's kids hamburgers
with French fries and CoCola
make his wife shrimps and whitefish
with bleu cheese on her salad
put him a steak on from off the bottom of the pile
I'll pay the different
Cookie said How he want that steak?
Miss Lela said Scriptural:
Burn that sonofabitch to Hell
and for the first time any one of us in our town
ever witnessed Missus Reverend Strayhan snorted
into her napkin then giggled into her chest
then broke wind into a belly laugh concerto that drew
Dryden's and Cecelia's at Alexander's Feast's Angel down
and though the Reverend swore a benedictory oath
of clearing he would never upon his life and precious
soul enter again that supper establishment
it never hurt Miss Lela's business not even one bit

Libretto: La Venganza Galleta Morena del Tejas
or
The Magnified Obsession

Io sangue voglio, all'ira m'abbandono, in odio tutto l'amor mio fini.
—CAVALLERIA RUSTICANA,
Pietro Mascagni
(based on the libretto by Giovanni Verga)

Based on an exhaustive, thorough, and complete
Folklore Case Study: Urban Legend Verification
The Authentic, True, and Original Version
Of the Texas Brownie Vengeance[1]

Matador, Texas 1957

Ruby Rushing said her first clue
was a knock on the door
with no post card or even telephone call warning
there stood a perfect stranger
telling two children holding on to her knees
Say hello now darlings
both hollered Hello Great Aint Ruby
ran past her like paired unbroken lapdogs hurrying
to be first to get through the door and into the house
then the woman reached out with a neck hug and air kiss
said It is so nice to see you again Aint Ruby
I hope we're not intruding stopping by
like you told me I should oughter do
anytime I'm in the neighborhood
when I met you at the House family reunion
right after I married LeRoy in 1949

I'm sure you remember me I'm Earlene
LeRoy's mama Mayhewn sends her love
said I could always depend on family hospitality
if I ever needed a place to stay the night
can you tell me where the bathroom's at?

said by the time she could get her situated
one of the kids had her snuff mop and
W. B. Garrett brown bottle in her hands
othern holding up the chair skirt
staring at one of the two spit jars
she had discretely hidden under the furniture
which she salvaged prior to incident
took into the kitchen pantry while they
began opening and slamming drawers
chasing each other through the house viva belezza vocale
asking if she had any toys they could play with
they were already beginning to feel bored

If it's anything we can do to help
with getting supper ready said Earlene
please don't hesitate to ask
sat down in Ruby's personal lounging chair
said It is so much further to Longview
than I remembered I am so proud
you live almost exactly half way back
could I bother you for a glass of ice water
or a CoCola if you happen to have one
how have you been since I seen you last?

said she sat on the furniture and talked
so much Ruby got a new interpretation
of the mystery of the Tower of Babble
while she fixed supper and set the table
got fresh towels and sheets from the chester drawers

made up the trundle for the boy
I hope it's no trouble Earlene said but I'd just as rather
we all three don't sleep in the same bed
Jimmy LeRoy tends to moan and waller
I do hope being in a strange house
don't cause him to have another accident
in the bed he's just a child
we caint hold some things against him
when it's only the fault of nature as we all know
kids pissed and whined about everything she put on the table
I'm not going to eat any of that
What is that stuff there?
This meatloaf tasties like it was raw liver oncet
You don't have to eat it then honey
Mama I don't want no supper can I go play?
of course darling remember not to run in the house
both raced straight to Ruby's bedroom slammed the door

Did you think to make any dessert
for these chirren they both have a sweet tooth?
sat on the dining room chair drinking her cup of fresh coffee
she asked to be fixed for her to settle her stomach
after her hard day of driving
to make it here while her aunt by marriage
cleaned off the table and washed the dishes
then said when Ruby was wiping
and putting them in cupboards
Would you mind much Aint Ruby if I went ahead
and pourn me a hot bath to soak in
so I can be ready to go to bed
after you get this all cleant up?
I'm just getting real tored from all the day's bidness
went and left her shelving leavings in the fridgerator

said it didn't even bother her that much
when she saw the children holding
the glass with her teeth night soaking
whispering about what they looked like
or when they piddled with her radio dial
she couldn't find any of her programs for three days
maybe a little bit or even more than that when they
got into her drawer with her S & H Green Stamp books
which she came in and put in the dishes cupboard
later the soup tureen with the lid on and then
caught Earlean with the door open
looking at the inside like something
might be of interest to her in there
but when she saw them playing with her chapsticks
they'd got out of the drawer in her room
right beside her bed on the table with the Bible
playing with the lids on them
she made them Put them back where they got it
then when she swabbed a splotch on her mouth
when she was putting on her nightgown
and knew they'd switched lids
put the white one on the tube for hemorrhoids
brown cap on the lip salve
later heard Earlene talking on her telephone
that night after she'd gone to bed and
Earlene thought she was asleep
telling LeRoy long distance on her number
what them little darlings had done How cute it was
they put their hands over their mouths
and run out the room so she wouldn't know
what trick they'd gone and played on her
Ruby said that was more than enough
for her to have to stand for and put up with
from family she couldn't have picked out of a crowd of two

far as she was concerned it was time
for the Comanches to put on warpaint

stayed awake until all three'd wandered through
her house and the ice box nine times each and gone to bed
for the night snoring and whacking and effluviating
went in to the kitchen and put on her apron
made a big pan of homemade brownies
with marshmallow pieces and dark chocolate syrup
twice sifted Pillsbury enriched flour and an egg
two cups and a half of sugar and a stick of butter
pecans smashed with a rolling pin
between two wash cloths and
folded into the dough and finally
an Eight Day melted bar of Super Strength Ex-Lax cubes
baked and cut into two inch squares in a wicker basket
with a blue gingham napkin for a liner
waited until after breakfast
where they wanted extra sugar on their frosted flakes
left the soggy bowls all half full on the table
they needed to be in a hurry
didn't even make up their beds because they Was sure
Aint Ruby would want to warsh them sheets anyways
the loading up into the car
hugs and air kisses and goodbyes and how
it would take another long day
of driving to get all the way back home
they'd be sure and tell Grandma Mayhewn hello for her
she said Wait a minute
I have a traveling present for you and them little darlings
a small something to satisfy their sweet tooths
went back and fetched the basket
brought and gave it to them through the window
said Wait till your mama says it's okay
before you eat these in the car

and be sure and save at least a piece for her
I hope you'll enjoy them as much
as I surely intend you will bye now
they drove off and left waving and hollering
who got the first piece

Coda[2]

seventeen minutes and eighteen seconds
after two that afternoon the phone rang
when Ruby answered it
Earlean House said Aint Ruby
is it any flu going round where you live at?
she said Why yes I believe it may be
I could have heard something about that
why would you be asking?
she said I'm thinking these chirren
might be coming down with virus
I just wondered if it could be
something they picked up along the way?
Ruby said That's a certain possibility
some of them flu's spread along nicely
Earlean said I wonder if I oughter stop
and take them in to see a doctor?
Ruby said Oh I doubt it
most of these childhood ailments I suspicion
only last two days or so more or less
then go away natural as it
works itself all out on its own
I wouldn't worry too much just yet
it's only the fault of nature as we all know
the Lord works in mysterious ways
you need to remember

He's always watching out for children and idiots
is our old family saying
you probley ought to get along on home
put them little darlings in their own beds
and you get all relaxed
have you a nice hot bath
from being wore down to a frazzle
after all that hard work
of getting reacquainted with the family in-laws
and driving yalls self all the way back to Longview
if it's any brownies left over
you just have yourself a nice piece
I think you've earned and deserve it
say hello to Mayhewn and bye now
hope yall had a real nice trip to remember

Notes

1. As told by Ruby House Latham Rushing to her daughters
Annie Sue Latham Wagner, Jessie Rushing Ivy Stailey Brown,
and Ruth Rushing Lee. Repeated to the Research Scholar/Poet-
Librettist by all three sisters on different occasions and retold by
his mother Ruth Rushing Lee after the two older sisters were
deceased.

2. Information in this section corroborated by Ossie and Evert
Smallwood, relatives of Earlene House and in-laws of Ruby
House Latham Rushing, on the occasion of their driving over
one hundred miles to the Lee home for Sunday dinner in 1960
without attending church services that morning after their
in-law Wheelis House had his teeth removed by a dentist in
Turkey, Texas, he accompanying them and complaining, "Ruth,
it isn't anything on this table I can eat," whereupon the Research
Scholar/Poet-Librettist's mother passed him the gravy boat, but

with a different interpretation of tone; from their point of view, the story, while true in factual data, was a betrayal of hospitality and an act of deliberate severance of ties established by marriage, leading to disinheritance, disavowal, and schism wherein she (Ruby House Latham Rushing), in their own words, "declared unpervoked war on her own family and in the eyes of the whole neighborhood turned the reputation of the House family into a pile of shit."

For my son
upon completion of all requirements
for his PhD in Folklore

Matthew 3:17

February 2009

Clean

Are your garments spotless,
Are they white as snow,
Are you washed in the blood of the Lamb?
        —CHRISTIAN HYMNAL NUMBER TWO

Cleanest woman who ever lived
was Missuz Bullard
her kids' ears bled she scrubbed so hard
even on Wednesday night prayer meeting
and after she washed clothes
in her house on Thursday
she'd use the washing machine water
to mop the porch and the sidewalk
and the street curb all clean

then her husband before he ran off
brought home this white cat
for the kids he named Nookie
so after she did those clothes and sheets
on Thursdays she's so clean
she washed that cat

it never left the house
but on Thursdays when she got out
the washing machine
you could see it through the window
trying to scratch a hole out
then by afternoon when she's finishing clothes
it'd be a white streak
across the floor one room to another

every one of her kids ran off and left
before they got out of school
and her husband with another woman
she still washed everything in the house
every Thursday and that cat
there was no chance for it to get away
she had one thing on her mind
and anything that was dirty
didn't have any place in there to hide

you'd hear her looking for it
hollering here Nookie Nookie, come here kitty
a block away you'd know
when she found it by the squall
her arms had scratch marks
all the way up but she never felt a thing,
by god, she and that cat were clean

Yet Another Reason

on Billy Jack Johnston opposing the gravelling
of city streets before the season of wind

He needs a jackass
to kick him in the mouth
and by god
I may just do it

From sidebar minutes of the monthly
Town Board Meetings
16 April 1957

Song of the Mill Worker

Dedicated lovingly to my fellow workers at Postex Cotton Mill,
makers and purveyors of Fine Garza sheets and pillowcases

The muslin cutter

7 a. m. Mill whistle, morning shift begins

I slit a sheet
A sheet I slit
Upon a slitted sheet I sit

I'm an old sheet slitter
The mother of a sheet slitter's son
And I'll slit my sheets
Till the next sheet slitter comes

7:01 a. m.

I slit a sheet
A sheet I slit
Upon a slitted sheet I sit

I'm an old sheet slitter
The mother of a sheet slitter's son
And I'll slit my sheets
Till the next sheet slitter comes

7:02 a. m.

I slit a sheet
A sheet I

Sewing machine shop

Oh my Lord
I caint bear the thought
of another day
singing rounds of
Row row row
your boat

Okay, Lorene
let's do something else
today then
Are you sleeping
Are you sleeping
Brother John, Brother John?

Spinning room

Godamitey it's hot

I think they turnt it up four notches

If it wadn't for the noise I'd think
about fainting of the heat
but nobody'd hear me fall

I swear it's hottern a outhouse in Hell

If I could I'd go to Hell

it'd be cooler there for sure

I wouldn't go to Hawawyah
if they gave it to me
I'm going Alaska my vacation

I'd go to North Pole

I'd go about anywhere
I could cool off

I got to get me a drankawater

Go head Sharon
I'll watch your looms
see if yougn find somebody
turn down the heat
Jesust God it's hot

You got it right there

HEY
Close that goddam door
you ignernt sonofabitch
This here's a control aviroment
you caint let that outdoor air in
we got to keep the tempature up
or the damn looms shut down
Was you raised in a barn
or what?

Muslin bleaching room

Bleach saturates the walls, ceiling,
floor, my clothing, the cloth, air,
my lunch pail, the time clock, my
hair, nose, eyes, between my legs
in my ears bleach permeates my life
wraps me in a swath of sour white
clings like a Jehovah's Witness to my neck
the sweat rivulets gushing streams
of bleach down my shirt, colorless stains
puddling the floor

> I told Harold don't you Ever
> bring a new white shirt home
> you have to have it you go
> to the Assembly of God Charity Store
> buy you one washed and ironed
> wear it three times and throw it
> in the trash can I won't do more

bleached fingers holding a cigarette
bleach in my sandwich, in my paper cup
Kleenex, napkin, toilet paper, comb
bleach that lurks under the rugs
in the dish towels, beneath my pillow
puddles and sourcurdles my dreams
bleach stuck in the throat like a liar's scream
the mortician's make-up on a drowned man's cheek

> I gave the daughters ten dollars each
> told them buy school clothes both
> brought home white panties in six packs
> I told them congratulations baby girls
> you just earned a tuition-free scholarship

in the art of hand-soap washing
a study that will last you a lifetime
you'll find a bleachless way
to keep them white and clean
words of profanity I will not tolerate spoken
in my home:

Clorox
Top Job
Purex
Oxybleach
Javex
Lysol
Oxyclean
White King
Zonrox
Green Cross
Biz
Oxyper

Lord give me color, a world rich in rainbows
no white bark trees or Cliffs of Dover
the scent of lavender and rosebush
frying bacon and onion and peach, apricot
cherry, garlic yes even liver, kidney
baked bread, marmalade and grape
yes Lord I will scuttle to the waft of pigpen
worksweat, tobacco spit and vinegar
and oh oh indeed Lord, if my job in Heaven
is the bleaching of angel's white robes
grant my living wish and send me straight
to a bleach free cedar fire scented Hell
with red and black robes and dancing Baptists,
indulgent Campbellites and filthy Nazarines
begrimed with the rich color of earthscent muck
and I, too, Lord, will forgive you every white thing

The palette stacker

Let me tell you something, Travis
woman to man as your Assistant
Personnel Director this one time
Hoyt there is in charge
of this entire mill's palette stacking
being a one man team
and if I were you which I'm not
I'd be careful about how
you've been talking to him
he's an odd duck and just doesn't
take to teasing any
and here's the consideration
I'm thinking I might take
if I were you which I'm not

that skinny little man
lifts 10 boxes of sheets every minute
and stacks them on his palette
that's 600 boxes of sheets an hour
which means in a workday
he lifts and stacks just about exactly
4,800 boxes of sheets
each box weighing 44 pounds exactly
which if you do the sum
comes to just a tad over
211 thousand pounds of lifts and stacks
on his palettes every day
five days a week and six
once we get to the holiday sale season

Travis, to put this in plain linguitch
as the good old boys say

so you might understand it
that skinny little man
who is from Shakeslovaskia
which is why to you he seems
to talk funny but he doesn't agree
has muscles in his shit
and if you tick him off making fun of him
bad enough to have him come at you
I can tell you for a certainty
the next one to wipe your butt
will be the undertaker

if you catch my drift

Shop

We have no Problems
We have Opportunities to Excell
　　　　　　　—framed motto on Shop wall

What do we got today?
2 broken foot pedals and
1 wore out bobbin in the sewing room
ladies must of got right rowdy
and racaucous singing rounds yesterday
we better get to that quick
or it'll hold up the whole mill works
1 replacement chain on the door lift
in machine storage
it don't need replacing
just a adjustment I'll bet you anything
sliding door off track on a B & O boxcar
I wisht they'd fix their own damn sliding doors
some of them boxcars hault Buffalo Bill
whyn't they get some new equipment?
fork lift needs a oil change and riser lube
Mayhugh whyn't you get on that?
florescent light out in the spinning room
goddam who wants to go in that loudass hothouse
where the ladies'll scream at you
to keep the dammed door shut
and put in a light bulb?
Cephas I'll give you a hour break
if you'll go do that for me
take whatall time you need on it
1 broke axle on a cotton bale dolly
Broke axle on a Cotton Dolly
how the hell'd they do that?

I never seen a busted one of them in my life
youg'n put a stick of dynamite
under a cotton truck and blown it
90 foot up in the air
it'll come down ready to go back to work
them things is indestructible
who was it done that?
probley dammed Travis Stribling
that boy could bust a self-winding wrist watch
setting in a Barcalounger
watching Queen for a Day
if Personnel had any sense God offered a goose
and got the lint balls out of their butt crack
they oughter fire him before he kills somebody
with our luck it won't be somebody needs killing
like him and his preacherly brother for instance
All right so let's take and get on it
before they bring in another list
is it Friday?
good deal Lucille
the eagle shits at 3 p. m.
excuse me Joan but I known
as well as you
you look forward to payday
much as any of us
What we standing around for?
whole dammed cotton mill
is awaiting for us to get it running
let's show em how it's done

The dock worker

J. C. Penny boxcar to Denver
12,000 full bed sheets, 8.000 twin sheets,
16.000 81 X 108 sheets

Stack those boxes
stack them high
stack them wide
81/108's left side back to door
stack them clean
stack them neat
stack them tight
floor to ceiling
stack them right
full beds right side
rear to door
twins we'll fill
along the wall
then close the door
stacking boxes
full bed twin bed
81/108 tight and high
neat and wide
lift those boxes
neat and tight
stacking boxes
high and wide
boxes stacking
back to door
stacking boxes
ceiling to floor
tight and wide
boxes boxes stacking

push them high
twin and full 81/108
stacking boxes stacking
high and tight
stack them neat
stack them wide
boxes boxes side to side
stacking boxes boxcar filling
tighter stacking boxes
twins against the wall
full bed right side
neat and tight
left side back to door
boxes stacking 81/108
boxes stacking
wide and high
stack those boxes
boxes stacking
clean and neat
high and tight
twelve more boxes
stacking 81/108
neat and tight
We filled that goddam space
we done it clean and neat
and high and wide
we done it right
Two more to go
before we quit tonight

Break time

All day every day
Larry Joe talks
Nonstop 7 to 3
All the women he's had
Looking for more

All night every night
Larry Joe talks
Nonstop to last call
At the Dew Drop Inn
All the boxcars he's filled

All the bedrooms
Larry Joe tells us he's made
High and tight, clean and neat
All those lovers doing it
On his loads of Garza sheets

3:15 p. m.

I'm home

How was work today, Hon?

Oh, about the same

Memoir: Church Social, 1959

We had summer picnic
out back of the churchhouse
that year it didn't even rain once
in June and what cotton sprouted
already gave up and died
nobody stayed home anyway
even Ellis Britton this one time
there was enough canned green bean salad
and gravy left over to feed out
Jesus' multitudes and a penful of shoats
with red beans and dabblings and green watermelon
because they had the party
too early for the ripening

so crowded nobody could find
a place to sit down together
half the family over here
the other half standing up over there
no shade trees
Hot godamitey Ellis Britton said
the men couldn't even crowd up and talk
about whatever's too important
for wives and children to hear
stood apart fanning with Baby Jesus paddles
or whatever they could find to shuffle the air
flies crawling across every face and neck
swat at one you'd hit Wayne Kiker's arm
dump a plate down his shirt
he couldn't even say dammit
would you watch out what you're doing?
because it was church house

Wallace Bradley said This is a little
like a class reunion aint it?
but the new Deacon T. C. Clark
who was desirous of the opportunity to be officious
and was also engaged in being high school principal
said No not exactly and Bradley
being huffy over the miffing said Why then?
to which Deacon Clark said Going to a reunion
is the re-meeting of old friends we may
be seeing for the very last time
while a church social is a gathering
of our potential eternal heavenly family
Lilly McCree the high school librarian and
Designated latitudinarian church intellectual said
The difference first being that meeting
an old friend requires the mandatory
deep peering into the former classmate's face
searching for the distinct signs of old age
poverty, sickness, and death
blooming like hideous noxious weeds
so we can say to ourselves
thank God I don't look that bad yet

And what after that? Wallace Bradley said
Stratifying success and discovering
that many lives have been disastrous failures
and the only option for that when self-realized
is to discover, track down and inflict maximum pain
on those deemed guilty for the fact
the real difference being that at a reunion
we are with people we will remember
while they are dying, wondering who is left
and here we are surrounded by people
we wonder if we even like and
simultaneously wonder if Deacon-Principal Clark

and the Pastor Strayhan are right
are these really the people we will spend
eternity with and is this the best we can do
Is that what you meant Principal Clark?
Wallace Bradley said and T.C. Clark
had to admit he didn't really know
which made Lilly McCree smile gleefully

Reverend Strayhan prowled around
shaking hands like election year
so much that Sister Stevens who we all thought
was the second oldest woman on earth
next to Missus Fortune said at our table
He took up and shaken my fingers
on such a multitude of occasions
I feared if he grasped my thumbs and pulled
they would give milk
Kristine Thornton said he better
stay away from her with a grip like that
his lovely wife wearing a new green dress
that seemed just awful out of season
for this year Betty Mason said
Missus Fortune said If he grint any more
he'd snap his jawbones
holding in his storebought teeth
down on his gums so they wouldn't fall out
when Hansford Hudman asked if he wasn't hungry
he said he wasn't in no hurry
he got whatall of the leftovers
he wanted at the end of the service
he needed to gather in his flock

Bretheren and Sistern and Ladies and non-members
of the Church said Reverend Strayhan
after he banged a spoon inside

a glass he poured out the icetea on the ground from
We've asked Brother Henry Wheatley
to offer the blessing on the food
so everbody bow your head
before the Lord's presence here today

at the children's tables Roy Don Staples
who already weighed 200 pounds
before he was twelve said
I can butter and put jelly on two light biscuits
chew and swaller them before he gets to amen
Emily Potts said No you caint
Jerry Nutt who was his best friend
said I bet you five dollars he can
she said You haven't got five dollars
he said Maybe not but you do

at the adult sitting table
Bart Landrum said almost out loud
Get a bite quick so you don't
starve to death before he gets
to blessing the sick and afflicted
private to his wife making sure anybody else
who wanted to hear it could
Henry Wheatley being an Deacon
had to set an example for the congregation
they knew it would be a long one

before he could get his throat
cleared so the Lord could hear
Billy Hill hollered Wait wait it's cars still acoming
we caint start the prayer yet
where is it some more tables to set up?
Mattie Evelyn Collier said Look in the Sunday School rooms
in the annex Billy Hill said Yall boys come help me

and most did except Charles Ivins who said he hurt his elbow
learning to play tennis he was afraid it'd be too painful
they found three more and chairs
while the cars parked and unloaded

Harold Rushing saw
those boys all carrying only one chair
he leaned and picked up a table each
under both arms said Foller me we'll get these set up nice
looked at Charles Ivins sitting down shook his head
said I thought Floyd Scott took off and left town
to be lazy in Sweetwater
he said I hurt my elbow
Harold Rushing said I can see that
it's the one you aint holding your head up on

set up the tables and chairs
Preacher said Brother Wheatley
would you offer the prayer now?
after everybody got situated back down
except for those standing
who didn't get any furniture
Lentin Ingram said Reverend
I believe I been Deacon longer
than Brother Wheatley
don't you think I ought to lead prayer?
Vera Gollehon who'd been County Treasurer once
and knew everything said
Harold Rushing's two weeks and four days
oldern you are I believe he ought to do it
somebody said How about Brother Stevens then
he's oldern both of them by half?
Sister Stevens said he'd rather not stand up
in the hot sun today he wasn't feeling too good
Reverend Strayhorn said That might be right

Vera Gollehon said It is for a fact
Lilly McCree said they'd probably argue
over it if the Reverend asked
Ellis Britton to give the malediction
Eulis Robinson said That's probably a fact
Ermine Thompson said Well
somebody ought to mention it then
but her husband Harold told her
it would be fine for her to let it go
so she felt slighted and got sullen
he said later for three days
Lilly McCree sat back and grinned into her napkin
knowing privately what she'd done
Harold Rushing stood up
everybody shut up and bowed their heads
he said Our Heavenly Father
Roy Don Staples said I can do three
and he did even before
Deacon Rushing got to the need
for a little rain if it'd be convenient

Amen he said finally
congregation commenced serious feeding
like eighty four hogs found the same garden gate
for a few minutes with ripe beets and cantaloupe
and new corn in their vision of heaven
the army of Christian soldiers marched
onward to do battle and make war on the enemy
named appetite

when they came up for air
Arlis Jamerson spoke first said Good god
who cooked that roastbeef
whoever it is I feel sorry for her husband
having to eat that

It aint the cook said Maypearl Hodson
meat's cut too low on the shank
got too much streffing it's a cheap piece
out of the worked over used meat bin
you caint even boil that soft
Just like this piece of stringy chicken
said Theona Josey
I think whoever brought this
fried up a stewing chicken
I bet some cow road killed
in the sun said Nolan Williams
they never had to waste no bullet there
Cut the bites littler said Cephas Bilberry
that way you can get it swallered
Jim Jackson the town butcher
sitting at the next table over
staring down at his plate
not anything taken off it
he's so astonished and admonished

nobody ate what they brought
looked around for something better
but wouldn't tell if it was
Mrs Buchanan the first grade teacher
said Longer I chew this the bigger it gets
R. B. McCravey said if he didn't
swaller his pretty soon he's gone have to
take his teeth out to hold it in his mouth
Ollie McDougald said he's afraid
if he et three bites of whatever it was they had
he'd have to untuck his shirt
his belly'd swolt up so much
Charles Ivins said there wasn't nothing
there he liked to eat was there any dessert?
Missus Fortune watched Roy Don Staples

load it in like the starving Armenian children
said Them Staples raised a true believer
that boy is turnt to the lard

Reverend Strayhan said Brothers and Sisters and young ones
we got a squatch of meat and chicken
and beans and salad and icetea
but we gone be short on pie and cake
because the Lord let it be too hot in His wisdom
for the wormen to turn on ovens
inside the houses for the occasion
so start planning your way around that

at the children's table
Roy Don Staples leaned across
to get a light roll off Joe Bob Trammel Jr.'s plate
because he ate his during the prayer
turned Monroe Newberry's drink
all over his plate and lap
he stood up with red kool aid
down his shirt front to his britches legs said
Well God damn Roy Don
all the kids transmogrified
most of them never heard him speak before
some wondered if he might be deaf
along with dumb after he failed fifth grade
Jerry Kuykendall said Monroe
you caint talk like that it's the churchhouse
you have to act respectable
Monroe said Na uh turned and walked off
stood in the parking lot by his daddy's car
in his new red speckled shirt
with the sunshine pouring down
like hell busted a gasket
wouldn't come back and eat

anything with the children after that

Will you look there Mavis Tittle said
when she saw Kim Pierce twisting around Jimmy Turner
in a real short skirt even the Deacons
couldn't help but notice
You'd think she'd of had more respect
than to show up at the churchhouse
looking like that she said
Naw said Carl Rains water here's
good as any for trolling
look over at that table watch them boys
squirm to get a sight line when she bends over
all accurately and exactly separated
puberty from childhood to test
their instinctive behavior by Kim Pierce's offer
of the golden rule opportunity

Lucille Thaxton who was being
the permanent seventh grade English teacher
substitute since they took Mrs Carpenter
back to the insane asylum at Big Spring again
and had her husband tell everybody
she was a intellectual giant
so she could take the opportunity to demonstrate it
stood up with her yellow hat that looked like
a Mason jar lid screwed on her head
said That is salacious and ludicrous
I shall have none of it let us begone Cyrus
him just sat down turning his plate
round and round to find a strategy
that could make it come out even tried to say
But Honey she said Now
we all could see she meant it with her head
flung back eyeballs pointed down on Cy

like God's wrath on the Ammonites or Catholics
had to get up and follow her off
with his napkin stuck under his belt
flapping like a string of toilet paper
hanging out the back

How does she do that? said Lester Williamson
Do what? said Odell Latham
Spread her mouth acrost her face
from behind one ear to the othern
then turn down at the ends
behind her jowls like a catfish I didn't know
a real person could do that
with its mouth could you? Ellis Britton
said he'd bet ten dollars
couldn't nobody else do it neither
then everybody at the table doing their best
even Mrs T. L. Jones who was second tier old
enough they said to been a witness
at the resurrection
embarrassed her husband
until he pulled out a ten dollar bill
gave it to her to make her quit it

all the children at their table saw
had to give it a try some held their breath
straining so their heads looked like balloons
trying so hard till they all yelled
Lookie Gayle Lynn See Gayle Lynn
Gayle Lynn Tittle looked like
her face was mashed in a washer wringer
mouth straight across all the way around
turnt down both corners more like a red snapper
than a catfish R. B. McCravey said

but admitted the effort
turned up a reasonable consideration

got up and ran over to show her parents
where her daddy was sitting campaigning to be Deacon
by the preacher's wife and Billy Hill
Mavis Tittle said What is it baby?
she showed her and she said
I'm real proud of you Gayle Lynn
Ollie McDougald said Hell of a thing
B. L. Wayburn said We all have to have
one thing or anothern
to hope for and believe in I guess
and we thought he was probably right

kids started hollering
Give her her ten dollars
Give her her ten dollars
Ellis Britton said he wouldn't
he'd made the offer as a wager
and chirren wasn't allowed
to be involved in gambling
so they should mind their own business
and stay out of adult affairs

We gone have a sermon
after this? Billy Edwards said
I don't think so but
we'll probably have a singing said Junior Potts
Mama said his daughter Emily
What baby girl? she said
Mama said Emily Roy Don Staples
farted at the table
What? said Junior Potts

Oh my said his wife
It wasn't enough cherry cake to go around
and he farted so nobody would eat theirs she said
Mrs Potts said Oh my again
Arty Gill said Did you give him yours?
Emily Potts said I had to it smelt too bad to eat there
he got four pieces and his fart stuck to the table leg
we all had to get up and leave
or it would get on our shoes
Oh my said Mrs Potts

Did you say it'd be a sanging said Modean Gill
Oh Lord is Kay Morris here? said Mrs Edwards
I'm not sitting by her if we sing
I'll do alto somewhere by myself
Hurry up and eat then we'll leave first Billy said
Me too said R. B. McCravey
Ollie McDougald said It'd be about like
the Reverent to pass the collection plate
after he never even brung
one bowl of food to eat at the party

whole congregation bent to the task
of consumption with Christian enthusiasm
to get it over with so they could go home
and turn on the swamp coolers
cars starting pulling out of the parking lot
like it was Talladega
Monroe Newberry directing traffic
praying and sweating it out
with everything he had in him
that he wouldn't become instant detritus
Reverend and Sister Strayhan standing alone
in the middle of Job's whirlwind asking
Where's everbody in such a hurry to go?

his wife staring around at the tables
and dirty dishes and spates of scrap food
asking Who's gonna help clean up?
nobody answered from the scuttle
or anybody told her what a purdy new dress
she chose for the occasion
the meeting had unanimously
been declared adjourned
without even a closing prayer

mama said that night
when she turned off the radio for bedtime
It certainly was fortunate members of our Church
were the only ones going to heaven
much as we all didn't like each other
or the weather or the praying and singing
or each other's cooking it'd be plumb awful
if the rest of the world had a chance
to make it up on our level too
and daddy who never was
much religious that we could remember
said Amen

Classified

I do professional quality FLORAL DESIGN if you will provide the materials and flowers. $1.50 to $5.00 per arrangement depending upon size. I am also selling some ORIGINAL POETRY which I wrote. Rights Included. And I do professional quality and HONEST HOUSE CLEANING. $1.00 per hour. No more than four to six hours per day at this time. No windows. I also do fine detail NEEDLEWORK pieces. No silk. Finished. In layed. Or unfinished. Can be used in a variety of size and detail. You provide fabric or buy my samples when available. You can contact me regarding any of the above between 9:30 A.M. and NOON; WEDNESDAY THROUGH SATURDAY at 68 NORTH 100th WEST STREET (the same street as North 1st West) REAR SINGLE SOUTHWEST APT. # S.E. (second of two doors. First is # A. Second and last is mine—# S.E.) Southland Texas. I have no go-betweens and no phone or message phone. ALSO, KITTENS (not for fund raising, experiments or bait) need homes. HUMANE TREATMENT a must. See only myself, MAVIS TITTLE, about all these matters

In a House Made of Time

Matthew 25: 14-30

Lucille Bullard was the best
wailer in the history of our town
also the first professional mourner
any of us ever knew about
she had the talent as a natural inclination
said it was a gift from birth
but diligent research enhanced her performance
read the Bible on sackcloth and ashes
went to John Wayne movies to see
Indian women cut their fingers off
tear out their hair
beat their faces up with their dead
husbands' tomahawks and billyclubs
so they could share their grief
with their women friends and children

most of it she already had in stock
she'd sliced the first two joints
off her pointing finger in a sausage grinder
when she was nine and her mother
cauterized it with a curling iron
put a bandaid on
said she wasn't going to waste
four pounds of sausage looking
it was gone for good
she'd already lost all her front
bottom teeth and one on the top at the side
in a fight with Leland Newberry at grade school
over whose turn it was to slide

her hair splotchy from ringworm scars
and with her fleshy weight all dresses
looked Pillsbury flour sack homemades

she learned her best effect passed down
in a legacy from Ruby Rushing
who picked it up when her husband Ike died
shared it with her nephew Wheelis House
who taught it to her at no charge
when she asked how he made it happen
swelling up his face till it looked
like it might explode with veins throbbing
both eyes puffed closed to bright red slits
he showed her how to bawl
into a steaming hot wet warshrag for fifteen minutes
to get the proper effect
done exactly right it would stick
up to three hours in public
she was willing to shake ashes
all over her if necessary
had the full repertoire of sound effects
crying to bawling to howling
to wailing at which she was world class
to shrieking that would draw banshees

tried it as an amateur at three different funerals
to test her sense of timing and volume
went to Rufus the undertaker at Mason's
offered services as a professional
best he could do at that stage was put her in
as an optional part of the first class gold package
starting at five dollars per memorial
thought she might be able to build up
income as her reputation spread

she might try the preachers
since it could wax into a crowd pleaser
fill up the seats with potential tithers

did some work with Reverend Strayhorn
then the Presbyters and Nazarites
so well for Kay Stokes' funeral
Scotty Sampson at the graveyard
wrote her a check for twenty dollars to do
his when the time came up
said he wanted the full spectrum
since he hadn't been able to locate bagpipes
lived fourteen more years during which
she perfected her performance and visited
him in the hospital when he was doing final preparations
about the occasion told him
she needed ten more dollars for inflation
since he was rich enough to afford high style
they argued for an hour before the nurses
called Dr. Tubbs to come get her
she was scaring the rest of the patients
he gave her five dollars and the nurses put in
the other five to satisfy her to go home and wait
Scotty Sampson bowed up and wouldn't go another penny
he said It was a matter of principle
Dr. Tubbs and the nurses didn't care
Jim Carmin had already said in public
both of them two's level was half a bubble off plumb
as an established fact

before that in the middle of her rise to fame
she became a legend when Coy Stribling
called and offered her twelve dollars if she would come
to the Church of God of Holy and Divine Prophecy and
    Revelation

and work Bill Gill's funeral because Coy
didn't know him and needed help
twelve dollars was almost half what he was getting
he'd never seen her regalia but heard
by reputation how she could make the difference
put her in the choir behind him
even if she didn't know the songs said
Join in whenever you think it's a good time
in full wardrobe including ashes
sat with her head down staring at the floor
so the only thing we could see was the top splotches
where her hair wouldn't grow back in

Reverend Coy did the requisite seven minutes
on the Lord's preacherly love for the church house
to a standing room only crowd when they found out
Lucille Bullard was performing
before he got to Bill Gill and his beloved family
recited scripture where God sayeth
He is the Alpha and the Omega
meaning the beginning and end of time
which meaneth God is time and we worshipeth
our Lord God in this church His House of God
where our beloved brother Bill Gill hath passed
over into the realm of light and time
cradled in the bosom of Aberham where he resteth
in Christ Jesuseth's folds and Lucille
took that as her cue to raise up from her scrunch
open her mouth where we could see
every tooth that wasn't there
her warshrag soaked eyes puffed up purple
in slits like a Yorkshire sow
sweat soaked ashes pouring down
her face like rivulets of mudwater

or blood if she was wearing a thorncrown
let out a bawl that modulated to a high wail
leaning up toward shriek
her neck quivering like a turkey wattle
or white headed Nebraska yodler
shaking so it might burst asunder as Judas's bowels
every hair left on her head risen to military attention
stood straight out in nine directions
waved that hand with the prominent missing finger
in the air and screeched

there were eight babies in that church house
just as well had been hooked on line
to a circuit board toggle switch
went off at once in a terror scream
all the fire trucks from Lubbock to Floydada would make
at the commencement call for the end of the world
each simultaneously turned and crawled up its mama
immediate verification which ones
had not attended to fingernails
three scratched like cats had climbed their necks
two appeared to be survivors of a rodeo knife fight
in possible need of transfusion
all joining the shriek and wail ceremony viva voce belcanto
    fortissimo
panic beyond the premises initiated by the pandemonium
dogs outside howled at a daylight moon
one screaming as if its foot was smashed by a tractor wheel
birds flew into house windows in flocks
to get away anywhere
children inside bawling under their beds
widows screaming the names of their forgotten husbands
husbands calling for their mothers
wives calling for their lapdogs and house cats

teenagers tossed out of their naps onto green linoleum floors
all the way to Main Street where people came out of shops
to see how many cars involved the wreck
Coy so shocked he reverted screamed
Jesust Christ so loud he was heard above the squalor
then slid back into the adopted method acting character
shouted Has returned among us
people standing up to see if the doors were open
the widow Mizrez Gill told Arty her son Slip up
look in that box and see if they was at the right funeral
him too ascairt to slip up anywhere said No
and he really meant it
then Lucille having achieved the supreme effect
leaned back in her seat in the choir
surveying her masterpiece
grinned like a participant on the winning side
in the first Parliament in Hell

Rufus said later it took every smidgeon
of every calmative lesson he learned
in mortician's school to first get Coy
then the audience and finally those babies
smoothed back down to ceremonial etiquette
didn't even let the Reverend finish his sermon
went straight to the benediction which he
behind the podium into the microphone delivered
nodded for the pallbearers to stand up
come get the coffin right then
closed the lid and wheeled it
through the attendant congregation
on the dolly out the door into the hearse
without even giving the opportunity to file by
and look at Bill Gill one last time

not truly dead but sleeping clasped
in the absolute surety of Christ Jesus's resurrection
turned and told Lucille Bullard
Get up out of that chair and go
out the side door right Now
don't do anything else today

for once in her life she followed
exactly to the red letter edition of the law
what she was asked to do
then when Rufus lifted his hands
like Charlton Heston parting the Red Sea
we stood and marched right up the center aisle
of the house made out of time
followed him and Bill Gill in the hearse
all cleansed and perfectly redeemed
in the blood of the lamb
by Lucille Bullard's consummate invocation
of the true essence of catharsis and fear of Coy's God
to Terrace Mound cemetery where Rufus put him to rest
out of the loop and that tragic masterpiece day
dedicated to eternal memory
finally once and for all

Another Reason Why You Didn't Want
Kristine Thornton
To Talk During Town Board Meetings

called out to Billy Hill
during a smoke break

I saw that girl of yours
wearing short shorts downtown yesterday
Deacon Hill
she's so skinny I told my husband
I couldn't tell if them were her legs
or if she was riding a chicken

From sidebar minutes of the monthly
Town Board Meetings
23 June 1959

Psalm of Home

Okay then, right here
Lord, in Bandera
Tether me to my shadow
Like a fat, spavined mule
Stuck sideways in Texas tankmud
Bawling for eternity

At midnight's closing whine
Of the 11th Street Bar's steel guitar,
When the stars slip their traces
And race the moon like wild horses
To their death in the darkness,
Let my hoarse song twine with the nightwind

May the bray of today's good laughter
Fall like a brittle topbranch
Windnudged from a sprawling live oak
Straight down like early spring sleet
To the hill country's bent
And trembling bluebonnet covered knees

Avenirse

Etymology/Diction
or
The Earthly Beatification of Miss Lilly McCree

She's the Lily of the Valley
Our bright and shining star
— variation on a recalled hymn
from my childhood

Lilly McCree rode herd
three generations on our town library
according to Ollie McDougald
taught every kid she met
what Mr. Twain said
He who will not read good books
has no advantage over he who reads no books
so even Goose Landrum
who was the embodiment of the second he
knew that maxim by heart
and gum chewing, whispering
or talking in the library was an abomination
answering to God Amitey at the Last Judgment

she became famous the first time
when Jiggs King got the Dispatch
to publish articles his Occupations Class kids
wrote as Spotlights on Workers in Our Community
sent Howard Lee Taft to do an interview
with Miss Lilly at the Library
then didn't bother to read over his essay
before it got submitted and published intact

Howard Lee started by asking
Was being a Liberian your first job you ever had?

she said Oh no
my first employment was as a waitress
at the Last Supper
he said Oh I didn't know that before
asked her to Go slow so he could
get it all wrote down in her own words
she made sure he did just that
so the whole town learned Bartholomew
he spelled Barnapple
paid the bill and Peter was Scotch
believed in only tithing
left the tip, a widow's might
and No she wouldn't truly recommend
waitressing as a Lifetime Occupation Choice
but she enjoyed liberianing
as it gave her the opportunity
to share her true love with both women
and men of all ages
who could read about it
as well as do it in person with each other
at the liberry or in the privacy of their homes
if they checked it out first

but the crowning pinnacle star in her halo
was bequeathed by our community
that day she stood face to chest
with Larry Joe Williams outside
the Church of Christ after services and handshaking
looked right up into his eyes
and clarified a principle
of temperament, language acquisition and usage
the entire near-monologue witnessed,
overheard and perfectly imprinted
on the memory synapses of three teenage boys
who interrupted their post-sermonic

philosophical discussion on the interpenetration
of truth, goodness, sex and football when Miss Lilly
opened her mind and heart that day

Larry Joe was neither loved,
liked, cared for, respected or preacherly tolerated
by anyone in our town
nevertheless a legend in his own mind
and his personal choice to be
Town Councilor, Mayor, Judge,
Justice of the Peace and Church Deacon
in the soonest possible order
as prelude to State Governorship
then perhaps a run for the Holy Grail
unseconded by anyone save his wife Laura
who spoke in such a still small voice
his self-nomination always declared itself
dead for lack of any known support
still he campaigned lustily and desirously
throughout the city from church pew
to Ingram's Barber Shop to the aisles
of Piggly Wiggly to Elder's Council
but hamartia's arrow flew into focus
when he attempted to address the issue
of his being passed over for Campbellite Deacon
inside the vestibule of the Public Library viva voce
only to be forcibly ejected out the front door
by Miss Lilly, a woman less than half his size
yet his equal in conviction and fortitude

still he persisted, even invoking Titus 1 dot 6
to remind the Elders' Council that T. C. Clark
had only One believing child
while he and his lovely wife
in the first four years of their marriage alone

brought forth four future proselytes
as the ocular fruit of his loins
not mentioning the fact of the first child's birth
occurring six months and seventeen days
after their wedding took place
or that his wife Laura presently carried
a fifth child as a result
of a prolonged evening of libations
in a futile attempt to procure acceptance and membership
in the Men's Glee Club at the Dew Drop Inn
items much discussed at the regular
monthly Eastern Star meetings
then taking the pulpit just before
closing prayer that memorable Sunday morn
to address the congregation regarding
the matter of his being passed over
once again in spite of his family's best efforts
he begged immediate intercedence
by his Christian brethren and sisters
in the matter of this unrighteous injustice
after which he walked up the center aisle
reserved for the preacher prior to benediction
to stand outside over by the pavement
and await their truly righteous sympathetic
condolences and outpouring support
to get this all turned around and made holy and correct
before God and the Public at Large

the only acknowledger
of his presence was Miss Lilly
who walked straight to his corpus
and first stared a direct line ahead
into the middle of his sternum
then lifted her face until she
peered straight up into his squinty Poland China eyes

said Larry Joe
while I may eventually be self-chagrined
for interrupting the exuberance
of your desire to be noticed
I want to offer you my sincere and humble thanks
emanating from every fiber of my being
and he said You want to thank me?
Miss Lilly said Wholeheartedly
Larry Joe said Well fine but how come?
she said All my life
I have engaged in a love affair
with the written and spoken word
devoted myself as Custodian of Culture
to honor the right literary, civil and genial
use of language which I have always
considered deity incarnate

until my contact with you
I believed we had sufficient wordage
such as malarkist, buncombe, vacuous troglodyte,
lambent dullard, cornaptious miscreant
all perfectly acceptable terms short of verbiage
for the socially and intellectually execrable
therefore I had never comprehended
manifest need for the coinage and usage
of the nominative cocksucker
prefaced by the adjectival stupid
to create what seems on certain occasions
the formation of a perfect inferior syllogism
until now
and thanks to you
I shall never again be confused
by that etymological necessity
for the immaculate riff-raffian appellation

for that I will remain in your debt
for a period of time extending into eternity

and then without waiting to hear
Larry Joe Williams say Huh?
Miss Lilly like neon Moses coming down
the mountain carrying the law in his pocket
walked to her 1948 Studebaker
in the Church of Christ parking lot
and drove home to *looke adoun ... and thenk on Christes passioun*
and eat her Sunday dinner, all alone, beatific

And Another Reason

during the debate on finding
a new town water supply

I don't know
how it is at yall's place
but the water's so hard
at my house
it's become a pleasure
to douche

from the sidebar minutes of the monthly
Town Board Meetings
13 August 1959

The True Story of Susan Birchfield,
Deputys Thibodeaux and the Texas Rat Snake

1

Susan Birchfield said the move
actually went better
than she expected
even though it took 432 trips
between the old house
and the new one on Silk Stocking
9 calls to the bank
4 to the preacher
1 to the J. P.
3 to the Joseys to reborrow
their big truck and trailer
and 2 to the marriage counselor
Dennis said before he'd move again
he would burn the house down
and start over
with or without insurance

Monday morning
him back at work
her time to walk through
just look it over by herself
with a cup of coffee
she felt good about everything
almost to the point of forgiveness
said she only meant
to look through the window
not at it
but right on top
of the drapes sprawled

like a three tawned housebroken cat
the six foot snake
proud to be an adopted
Birchfield family member

she remembered saying out loud
I can live without that
said she did not spill
one drop of her coffee
on the carpet or table
set it down
turned and picked up the phone
called the Sheriff's Office

Sheila she said
I need some help here
at my new place
Sheila said Is it a disturbance, maam?
Susan said Yes I believe so
Maam is it an intruder? Sheila said
Susan said Oh yes I believe so
Are you in danger, maam? Sheila said
Susan said I might be
but not in an immediate manner
Sheila said Maam, I'll send
Deputy Sheriff Thibodeaux
as soon as I can find him
Susan said Start at the coffee counter
at Adolph's and ask Laurie if he's there
Sheila said Yes maam I'll do just that

2

Yes'm Deputy Sheriff Thibodeaux
said when Susan Birchfield

opened the door after he rang the bell
I understand you have a disturbant
on your premise
she said Yes I do
he said Maam I understand you
have a intruder here at you house
she said Yes I do
he said I be here
to be of assistant
what can I do to help, me?
she said You come right this way
took him in to the living room
pointed at the window

he looked through it hard
to find out where it was hiding
whatever it was
until she put her hand in front
pointed his face up
said it took about nine seconds
of looking to see what he was seeing
said Holy Mary Mother of Got
blessed be the fruit of the loom
on baby Jesust
pulled out his pistol
hollered You stay right there
don't you move
she yelled No no
put that gun up
don't you shoot that
in my house
said his eyes could have been milked
if you'd grabbed and pulled on them
he was ascairt
said It's a snick up there

she said Yes it is
can you get him down?
he said No ma'am
I shoot him off there for you, me
I don't touch no snick
it be dangerous

stood right there in that room
like Lot's wife
looked at that snake
sleeping on top of the drapes
for a long time
pointing his pistol at it
she telling him four times
Don't you shoot that gun
in here you hear me?
he said finally You got any telephone?
she said Yes of course
he said I needa use it
mebbe I call my cuddin
he been to Snick School
he know what to do
she dialed the number
while he held the phone
with one hand
pointed his pistol at the snake
with the other

said LeRoy you get in you truck
drive you self right down here
to new Birchfield place
on Silk Stocking
where you see
my patrol car park

bring you snick catcher
we got us a problem, Houston

3

Mizrez Houston,
Assistant Deputy Constable
LeRoy Thibodeaux certified
in snaik removal at you service
how can I hep you? hidy yall cuddin Jodean
Howdy doodey LeRoy said Deputy Thibodeaux
My name is Mrs Birchfield Susan said
LeRoy get in here and lookee
we got us a problem Deputy Thibodeaux said
you got you snickstick?
Right here said LeRoy
walked in past Mrs Birchfield
without being invited
into her living room

Jesust Thibodeaux
LeRoy said when he saw it
that's a damn water mosacin
I think yes
You think so? said Deputy Thibodeaux
Mebbe a dimentback I think mebbe
Aint got no rattlers I see
Could be a giant coppermouf
I dunno
it's one damn big snaik
I can see yes, me
mebbe one them amaconda
crawl up through the sewerpipe
bite wormens on the butt

set and stare up
through the toirlet said LeRoy
Where they come from?
said Deputy Thibodeaux
I think Brasil down south somewhere
they say said LeRoy
That's a long way off to come
to bite a womern on her butt
said Deputy Thibodeaux
That's why they crawl
through the pipe
come out and eat babies
at night and crawl back in
how come you got you gun
out point at me
coonass? said LeRoy

I shoot that sonofabigsnick
he come after me said Deputy Thibodeaux
Don't you shoot that gun
in my house said Susan
Only if he come offer to bite on me
said Deputy Thibodeaux
Not in the house she said

What you gone do
Mr snickman now?
said Deputy Thibodeaux
We got catch this snaik
put him in a bucket
with a lid on it said LeRoy
You got a bucket with a lid?
said Deputy Thibodeaux
No you? said LeRoy
Hell no what I need a bucket

with a lid on it for?
how come you call me
coonass you peckerhaid?
said Deputy Thibodeaux

You got a bucket
with a lid on it Mizrez Houston?
said LeRoy
My name is Mrs Birchfield and there's
a soap bucket with a lid
in the laundry room said Susan
Would you axe Mizrez Houston then
if we could borrower that bucket
for mebbe little while
catch this snaik? said LeRoy
I'll go get it said Susan
You shouldn't call me peckerhaid
talk that way in front
of the wormen
who wake heah said LeRoy

4

What we do now? said Deputy Thibodeaux
You take this snaik stick
put the catcher on that big snaik haid
pull him down and put him
right in the bucket
I put the lid on then
said LeRoy
You the snickman
been to snick school
you put the snickcatcher
on his head I hold the bucket
Deputy Thibodeaux said

Aint what I train to do
I train to put the lid
on the bucket
after you put him snaik
in the bucket yes said LeRoy
I aint traint catch no snick
said Deputy Thibodeaux
That aint part of my job no

Go head said LeRoy
aint no problem
big one easy to see
what you doing
put snaik catcher right up there
catch him behind haid
pull he down and put him
in the bucket
Hell no said Deputy Thibodeaux
I aint touch no snick

Here said Susan Birchfield
give it to me
lifted the snake stick
up to the curtains
slipped the loop
over the snake's head
pulled it down
off the drapes
to the floor
where it sprawled
like an overfed pig

Gotdam lookee that bump
in his belly he done et sumin
mebbe somebody's baby

said Deputy Thibodeaux
No aint that big said LeRoy
I think me mebbe somebody's
little dog mebbe cat yes
It's a mouse said Susan
It's not big enough to be a dog
I think you right ezactly
Mizrez Maam said LeRoy
You better get him in a bucket
before he wake up hungry again
hold he up and put him in

Got him haid in said LeRoy
Jodean you put that damn gun down
put him tail in the bucket
I put the lid on
Hell no said Deputy Thibodeaux
I told you oncet and twicet
I aint touch no snick
Not gone hurt you said LeRoy
She got his haid down Mizrez Birchhead
Mizrez Birchfield said Susan
Hell with haid said Deputy Thibodaux
I shoot him right here
in the bucket
Don't you shoot that snake
in my bucket in my house
said Susan You put that gun up
I aint touch no snick
said Deputy Thibodeaux
Here she said Hold the snake stick

gave it to Deputy Thibodeaux
in the hand without a pistol
picked up the snake's body

wound it like a rope coil
into the bucket
Put the lid on LeRoy
Deputy Thibodeaux said Put it on now
I caint LeRoy said
Snaik stick he's in the way
you got to get it off
Get it off? said Deputy Thibodeaux
Yeah you grab snaik's haid
and take it offen, you

Here, said Susan
hold still
I'll do it
You be careful now
Mizrez Houston
LeRoy said
You don't be letting
him bite you any
I won't said Susan
Would you please
get out of the way Deputy Thibodeaux
I got the lid all ready
said LeRoy
When you get him off
we'll be all done and finish
pretty soon now all right
Don't let him get away
said Deputy Thibodeaux

5

Here you bucket maam
said Deputy Thibodeaux
we done toin that snick aloose

like you said we do
Did you shoot that snake
Deputy Sheriff Thibodeaux?
Susan said
No maam
I couldn't hit him
with no pistol
he done gone off somewhere home
out in the wood by hisself

I want pologize for my cousin LeRoy
he sometime got
a filfymouf on him
he don't mean nothing by it
he tell me he tell you
tell Mizrez Houston herself
you better warsh this bucket
out real good
for Mizrez Birchwood
before you used it
it got a whole lot
of snickhaihr in it
Oh yes, I will do that
said Susan, indeed
Yes maam said Deputy Thibodaux
I suspicion you will
do that about ezactly

and then she said
so she could get it
exactly right in his own words
as he might of said it
Without adieu or au revoir
he got in his patrol car
to went and left

the premise
to look for him
a hot cuppacoffee
and somebody to tell
all about his day
about the bigamuch one
he toined aloose
and let him get away

Eloise Ann's Story: Upon Her Daughter
Finding the Shotgunned Bodies of a Sandhill Crane
and her Colt in the Grainfield Stubble

I remember when I was her age
one of our neighbors shot my puppy
Daddy said He will pay for that in the hereafter
down the road from our place
somebody had painted on a sign
              Repent
        Jesus is coming
              Soon
        The end is near

and I thought then
no it isn't
either it's already come and gone
and He went away, left for good
or it's too late
we are all sunsucked dry with meanness
where a bucket of water on cheatgrass
wouldn't pull enough suption
to let a stem call up spit

why would He want to come back to this?
that's what I wanted to know
what I had to say about all of it back then
when I was a child like her wondering
why somebody would do something like that
to my puppy dog, to me
to my whole world and everything
I'd learned to believe in
about it all

The Longest Public Speech (of a Lifetime)

What I don't like, Rita Jean Ledbitter said to Larry Joe Williams,
is people who come to the Dew Drop Inn
just to hold court and change every subject
to something about hisself
and what I really don't like is people
who think they know more than God
about anything that comes up
in spite of the fact that the hardest
three years of their life was fifth grade
and what I really really don't like
is people who look around the room
when they walk in to see who's not there
so they'll know who they're going to talk about
and repeat a conversation
that never on this earth actually happened but
He with a capital H meaning you with a actual little y
happened to be just exactly right about it all anyway
and what I don't like most, very most of all
is people who piss me off to where I have to first swear
and then have to make a speech about it
when I'm more afraid of talking in a crowded room
than I am of going to Wednesday night prayer meeting
after eating purple speckled butter beans for supper
so I'll be able to go to sleep tonight
and not have to lay awake
thinking about what I wish I'd said
which I now won't have to do on this night
so I want to thank you from my heart's bottom
for being the kind of precisely rotten sonofabitch
who can provoke a decent night's sleep for the likes of me

and for that I wish you a most wonderful eternity in Hell
in a room all by yourself with only a mirror to talk to
so you will surely think you wound up in Heaven
and that I will therefore feel no guilt whatsoever
for persuading whatever gods are listening
as to the situation and terms of your final
secure and permanent encapsulation
good night and sleep tight, little boy
don't worry about bedtime prayers
they done been all said for you
And that's all I have to say
Clovis, I'm ready
to go home

now

Summer Solstice

The Temple of Shiva, Lord of the Dance
so dry, so hot the Mexican Hats
are hung over
Firewheels bloodshot, interwoven
with Cheatgrass and Bermuda
Mexican Petunia, perennially unwanted yet reborn,
spit their seeds across rocky soil
insistent in the desperate attempt
at significance and endurance

Beneath a bare knuckle sky
tangled within a thirststarved Live Oak
a Cardinal wilts inside her plaited nest
like a virgin martyr
trapped in the web of pyre faggots—
the blistered and windbled earth
smolders in the calloused palm
of the Sun God's raging mind,
rolls its chained journey into flame

The Fish

... victory filled up
from the pool of bilge
where oil had spread a rainbow ...
... until everything
was rainbow. rainbow, rainbow!

—Elizabeth Bishop, "The Fish"

Arty Gill went down
to the cafe that Saturday morning
to have coffee with the boys and that's all
until he found Cephas Bilberry and Roy Talbert
ready to go fishing and he knew
that's what he wanted to do more than life
even bought an extra case of Lone Star
so they could make sure they all had good times
he was happy as a goose
that found him a half pound of raw bacon
his wife Modean had to call B.L. Wayburn
at 10:12 that morning waiting long enough
for him to get done and back home for chores
to find out where he was
didn't even come home to change his clothes
only thing she'd told him he had to do
that day was fix the shelves in the closet
and clean out the storage shed
so she could get to the canning jars
with maybe one or two other odd jobs needed doing
he was going to hear about it
when he got back for sure
B.L. Wayburn said he expected that to be a fact

didn't get home until after dark
all three chasing beer with whiskey
thirty-two fish in two towsacks
a pound or better one catfish
upwards of six to eight they bet
poured them all in the kitchen sink
went to the living room
sat down on the furniture to tell each other
how it had been catching them fish
one more time until they all three
went to sleep sitting up in their chairs
except Arty laying on the long divan
Modean never even came out
of the bedroom to look at the fish

woke up about three in the morning
to pee bad all that beer moving
Roy Talbert in the bathroom
being sick with the door locked
Arty couldn't wait he went to the sink
there were all those fish
his wife hadn't even cleaned up yet
said the smell of it almost turnt his stomach
made him so mad he's ready
to knock down that bedroom door
make her get up and do those fish right then
had to hold them apart with his hands
all sticky and smelly so he
could see to hit the drain hole
if he hadn't been so dizzy from the whiskey
he'd have brought it all to an end right then
he had to lay down room was circling him bad

when he got up Sunday morning
bedroom door still shut

he could tell she'd come out
about had a brain spasm when he saw
that trashy woman had made her breakfast
piled the dirty dishes after eating
right on top of all those fish
laying goggle-eyed waiting to be cleaned

he had it went right to that door
said Modean you in there?
jiggled the knob to see it was locked up
said You come out here right now
get this kitchen all cleaned up
you beginning to embarrass me
saw Cephas and Roy Talbert staring at him
waiting for her to come put coffee on
said Come on out of there Modean
no sound from that door
smacked his hand on it flat said
You get on out here right now
get these goddam fish and dishes out
of this dirty sink and in the frigerator
you listening to me?
still no sound said
You testing my patience I'm warning you

she said then from inside the room
I'm not touching those fish Arthur
you can do whatever you and the two men
sleeping in there with you drunk
want to with them they're yours
he said You say what? hollering by then
said You heard me
I'm not coming out there until
you've got that kitchen all cleaned
like it was when you came home

forty-two minutes and eighteen seconds
after eleven o'clock last night drunk
he said Modean it aint my job cleaning no kitchen
with your dishes I never messed up
you come out that door
she wasn't talking by then
went in and sat down staring back
at Cephas and Roy Talbert
neither one offering any advice for once
just wanted coffee like it was supposed to be
hollered finally They'll lay there
a week before I'll touch them
real low heard her say Fine
he said Two weeks by god
real low again said
You are drinking up your prime water
made him mad as a wagon
to be talked to that way in front of his friends
whether they were drunk or not didn't matter
jumped up and ran to that door smacked it
with his fist screeching like a hog being nose-ringed
You open this goddam door right now
I'm gone bust it off its hinges
stepped back and lowered his shoulder
bunched up to butt it down

door might as well have been invisible
or made of glass
they heard the bolt side open
sound of a shotgun shell
pushed in the breech
then the bolt closed
like it was right there
in front of all six eyes open not blinking
Arty on one foot getting ready

to rooster fight that door frozen in ice
Cephas and Roy Talbert putrified
on the front of their chairs
then like an icicle melting came back
set his foot down
turned his head back at them
said I believe she's ascairt enough
maybe I better let off the pressure
they both said they believed he was exactly right
wasn't no use to even talk about it
they better get on home now it's late
went out the front door
without even dividing up the fish

said he couldn't stand it in there no more
all that cold air and dead fish
put on his hat and went
to the cafe for his coffee
wouldn't even talk to anybody about it
because they hadn't found out yet
when he got home she was gone

pushed him one too far he said
made him some breakfast and threw
his dishes in there with hers
on top of the fish in the sink
then dinner and supper when she
wasn't back from running off yet
including bologna rinds and bread crusts
he put water on so they'd stay soggy
slept on the furniture by himself
so when she snuck in late she'd see
he wouldn't sleep in that bed
with or without her by god
it was now a matter of principle

third morning he got up and looked at that sink
flooding over with dishes and garbage and fish
got so mad he stood in the kitchen and hollered
at her by name for ten minutes
then ran to the sink and started throwing
everything in it out on the floor
fish stiff and crooked
all but one he couldn't believe it
that big catfish on bottom still alive
buried under there waiting
its mouth going open and shut gasping
for clean air as much as he was
threw it on the floor and watched it flop
walked out the door and went to the cafe
had to sit by himself at the counter
had the fish smell too bad in his clothes
even Tommy Minor who was a slow child
had a hard time walking by him
didn't even hide it was a task worth wages
Arty walked a path around the fish
all the rest of the week stinking
had to open all the windows
to let air in and out

drove to Tahoka on Sunday
to see if she might be over there and give
her opportunity to apologize if she'd had enough
nobody had heard of her they said
Monday he couldn't take it any more
went in to look at the fish flyblown and oily
thought he'd proved his point
it was almost a week and a half
studied for nearly an hour in the door
called Huffman Furniture to see
if there was any way they could come out

lay a sheet of linoleum over the top
mash it all down in between
Victor said he'd send Ardell down
next morning but when he came he said No
there wasn't any way that'd work
he'd have to get it all up first
Arty said What will you take to do it?
Ardell said he didn't need no money
that bad yet he'd have to pass

Arty called every housecleaner in town
starting off with Xochi Valdez that day
they all said No they wouldn't
word got out most wouldn't even talk to him
on the phone said they weren't home and wouldn't be
for a long time more like his wife said
he was on his own

must of urped upwards of a dozen times
during those latter days when he wasn't lying
any more calling in sick to work
they seemed to know it
came to the cafe they wouldn't ask
just brought him thin soup and coffee
at the end of the counter with the door open for air
even Roy Talbert didn't sit with him
we wouldn't have thought he'd notice

Friday went in with a grain shovel
and a sheetrocker's gas mask on his face
in that kitchen with the house opened
scraped up everything that hadn't melted in
the floor and threw it out to his pickup
in a barrel so rotten it ruined it to the point
he couldn't even haul pigfeed

drove it out to the dump ground
where they made him pay four dollars
to unload in the dead animal pit
and then told him he couldn't
even leave the barrel there
had to crawl back in and pour it out
haul it over to the landfill
so they could cover and bury it up

went home poured coal oil and turpentine
ammonia and Turtle Wax mixed with fly spray
on that floor until it looked like gravy
washed it out the door with a water hose
did it again twice more
said if it didn't get it out that last time
he was ready to burn it down with or without insurance
washed up all the dishes he hadn't ruined
took his smelly clothes to Isaacson's Laundromat
gave the girl six dollars to run them through
as many times as it took to get
Every bit of that fish smell out with Clorox
went home and took a hot bath
with half a bottle of shampoo
four squirts of Wildroot hairoil and a bottle
of lemon juice with Bab-o stirred in the water
to get it out of his system

at the cafe they all said
he looked to be a new man
let him have his coffee in the booths
with the real people up front
said he couldn't eat yet and it might be a long time
before him and his appetite could get back on speaking terms
he was just glad to be alive
wouldn't never again wonder how

it might be to live with Wesley Stevens
or be one of the Bullards

came home he couldn't believe
whether it was a vision or the devil
Modean in the kitchen standing by the stove
cooking supper in fried grease on top
said his knees went loose and he retched out loud
at the thought of fish frying
or being cooked in there in any fashion
she said Wash up if you're going to eat supper
he couldn't take any more suspense
or tragedy in his life that day
held his breath and leaned in to see
beans in a pot and fried potatoes in a pan
and a cut up chicken in that boiling grease
it was almost enough to make him think
he could ever be in love with a woman like her again
changed his mind on the spot
didn't make her apologize in public
for her misbehavior and negligence

said it wasn't worth it
it was all water under the boat in the past
he'd learned a lesson to be learned
never again would he ever
bring home that many fish to lay in the sink
more than one night before he'd find a way
to get the neighbors to take some
even if he had to pay them to do it
and trying to find something like that
to get out of cleaning the storage shed
was not in any recognizable or memorable way
worth a new two hundred dollar kitchen floor
to save what's left of his

not very good in the first place marriage
sometimes it's best not to fish or cut bait
but just get the chores all the hell over with

Piggly Wiggly

Checker is beautiful
dark, shiny hair
—Herbert Scott, GROCERIES

When we ran short on community pride
as occasionally happened
we could always turn to our local treasure
Hooter Hagins who we all knew
without more than minimal doubt
was quite possibly the finest
grocery checker in the history of the universe

she hated algebra even more
than the rest of us in high school
for her it wasn't even the teacher
Mr. Tittle's breath that wilted plastic flowers
she hated writing out the formulas
with the transferring pluses and minuses
when she could do it in her head
like she thought anybody
ought to be able to
with any modicum of sense at all

take the Friday problems test
she'd sit and think about it
for a while then write the answers
he'd tell her she had to work
all the formulers out on paper
she said How come?
he said So I can see you not cheating any
and understand the algebraic process

she said How could I be cheating?
you give me the question
I told you the answer
I don't see I need any algebraic process
I was born with a good process
for me the first time
he didn't like that one bit
since he was also a promising
gospel preacher and took it
in a personal born again light
but had to admit she could do it
even though he didn't know how

she would add up groceries
on the register without looking
at her fingers moving over the keyboard
do a running total in her mind
while talking to you about the weather
or which bootlegger had the best
current supply or who
deputy Sheriff Junior Shepherd
was trying to get in the sack this week
or what her opinion was
on Reverend Strayhorn's latest obsession
or Coy Stribling's current idiocy
when she pulled the tape up
check it with her arithmetic
if it didn't add up it was always
because she missed a finger button
or that damn Byron Hainie mismarked
another can not paying attention stocking
she'd catch it either way
inside her mind

always have something nice to say
even to the ones she had every right
to wish were dead in their graves
on the sorry end of the cemetery
or married to Wesley Stevens
we'd all try to get in her line
even when it was stacked two back
over Penny Raines' just to have her
act like we were her pretty near best friend
she hadn't seen in such a long time
we all still think she invented
Hope you have a nice day

Junior Potts' wife
brought it up in the Ladies Church Social Hour
that it might be a potential disgrace
her having two divorces already
not even thirty or forty yet
now taking up with that foreign
out of state newcomer from Arkansas
maybe they ought to call her in
talk to her about community standards
got in her line at Pigs anyway
with her little girl Emily
Hooter did her groceries
like she was Mrs. Jesus Christ all smiling
said Why Miss Emily
I believe you are the purdiest young lady
I've about ever seen
if I was as purdy as you
I could already of had four
different husbands by now
Mrs. Potts about had a spasm

of embarrassment
only thing she could think of to say
was to Emily to Tell Miss Hooter thank you
Emily said I'm four years old
held up her fingers to show
Hooter said That is real fine baby girl
I am just so flat tickled proud of you
that'll be fourteen dollars and
sixty five cents please
I'll get your green stamps Mizrez Sister Potts
who couldn't even make her mouth
work to say Thanks so much only nodded
when Hooter told her she hoped
her day would be real real nice

but the one that was legend
was Mrs. T. L. Jones checking out
always took her eight minutes
and fourteen seconds to write a draft
after she'd gone over the cash register slip
three times to make sure she
hadn't been cheated on anything
then counted every green stamp
to make sure they came out even
Hooter still said Have a nice day
Mrs. T. L. Jones looked straight at her
said No thank you
I've made other plans
Hooter leaned out to her personal
said Well by god I hope you
give him something to remember it by
for one damn sure long time then
Mrs. T. L. Jones had to take a step back
away from her to digest it
without even a mortician's grateful smile

said You can be damn sure of that
Hooter said I don't doubt it
not even for a minute
Mrs. T. L. Jones said I don't blame you
and then Hooter said Good luck Mrs. Jones
I surely wish you well
and without another word
Mrs. T. L. Jones sucked in her breath
got her groceries and went and left
to get on with her private business
our whole world by Hooter's officiousness
now alerted and on point to monitor

And One More Reason

*to Reverend Strayhorn when he protested
the new home-ec. teacher lecturing her students
on human reproduction*

You preacher people
with your Peterless
non-existent Pearly Gates
think all the rest of us
are somehow worried that
we're locked out forever

*From sidebar minutes of the monthly
Town Board Meetings
25 February 1960*

Hooter

and down they forgot as up they grew
—E. E. Cummings,
"anyone lived in a pretty how town"

1

Back in the once upon a time days
Hooter Hagins got to be famous
a lot longer than the rest of us
but until Maurine Huffman
told her story to her Bobby Jack
almost everybody
even those of us who knew her then
and were there had already forgotten
that we all thought
it was a miracle
or a terrible accident
She had only one breast
 No one was ever really sure
if they had to take it off
when she was a baby
or if she was born that way
and nobody ever thought
to ask her or her mama
which was what
to resolve the dilemma

none of us seemed to notice it
until we were in junior high school
on a day like a bolt of thunder
Monroe Newberry who was so innocent
he didn't know any better

made the longest speech of his lifetime
when he said Jesust Hooter
you only got one tiddy
from then on as long
as we could remember to think
about it she was
as important to our self identity
as President Eisenhower or Sputnik
or Governor Shivers or Coach Darrell Royal

in high school it seemed
she'd managed to find a way
to get it centered so we could look
forward to sweater days
to see Hooter's point of view
then along came Ella Mae Blodgett
with snow cone brassieres
Hooter got one to work for her
so well that Mr. Bennett
in general science quit
trying to teach any at all
on those days and had work sheets
in his drawers
ready to pass out so he
could practice on his personal theory
of successful sight alignment

wore it to class next semester
on biology test day
after ten minutes Tommy Bouchier
who was a Baptist and refrained
from all lustful contemplation
until he went to college
got up and walked out
sweat running down both sideburns

took it in the library after school
on his own time and still
graduated class valedictorian
nobody could hold
any of it against him

2

years later at the Dew Drop Inn
across the tracks drinking
bootleg liquor Jimmie Ivie asked
Bus Pennell how he lost his eye
Was it a hunting accident?
which gave Bus the opportunity
for personal loquaciousness
he said Partially
it was on a Saturday night
in my pickup out in the bushes
with Hooter I goosed her
she jerked aloose
her gazoobie was like a brick
with a carriage bolt
stuck in the end of it
tore it right out of its sockets
he should have laughed
at the end of his story
and reminded them of what
they'd misplaced in their remembrance
that Charlotte Paducah before
she married Bobby Joe Rushing
shot it out with a Chinaberry
in a slingshot
when he came into her yard
after she told him not to
but when he didn't

went as quiet in there as when
Jerry Banks puked in church
during communion service
after Charles Ivins told him
it was made out of dead
ground up body parts
he wouldn't put it in his mouth
and be a cannibal
Miss Lela's eyes all wide
because her mama was midwife
saw it at Hooter's birth
them people didn't know
if it was from the Lord or the Debbil
but she had surely been touched
way back before Bus Pennell
got to her in his pickup
rumor of it spread all the way
to Odessa we heard

3

we were in line
at the picture show on a Saturday night
somebody
we later thought Wheelis House
brought his cousin
down from Tahoka to go to it
he'd forgotten to warn him
the potential consequences
of silliness in our town
he said too loud
Looks like a Chinese rhinoceros
yall ought to call her Ichiban
like that Jap wrestler in Lubbick
Harold Wayne Clayburn said

You want us to call you a doctor
or a vegetarian? he said What?
never saw a thing
she hit him holding a half drunk
R. C. Cola bottle with peanuts in it
on the point of his chin
went down in a squatch
like a jellyfish
that lost its bonnet at sea
one eye rolled up and the other one
looked straight out like it'd
been painted on
knocked him right out
of one of his shoes
she said to Harold Wayne
It's a veteranarain dumbass
whoever it wases cousin
that brought him
probably Wheelis
tried to say He didn't really
mean nothing by it
but Glenda Hutto
who was her friend that night
beside her standing in line
said It's too late already
you don't call the roofman
when it's araining

we heard all over town
that at the Rotary Club meeting
Pastor Brother Gene said
It was a stampede
of accumulated wisdom and grievance
that she chose to unleash
upon that poor foreign boy

at that very moment
in order to provide the incentive
and momentum for possible redemption
and on the other hand
he probably just should have stayed
at home in Tahoka that night
even though they all laughed
it was standing room only
at the Methodist Church
next Sunday in anticipation
that Hooter might show up
for admonishment or praise

4

she began to disappear
from our collective consciousness
when she married down horribly
to Paulie Joe Wheaton after
he came home from his two years
Army service in lieu of the penitentiary
then another divorce after him then
married Byron Hainey who drifted
on the lam from Arkansas
got him a job at Piggly Wiggly finally
sacking groceries and stocking shelves
by then time and gravity
had done its duty
along with cancer getting popular
and other women getting one
or both of theirs cut off
so it wasn't much unusual any more

we forgot about her mostly
until the new husband we never accepted

either for us or her
got the prostrate cancer
took him to Dr. Tubbs
who called in Hooter
the first time said Your husband
is a real sick man but
would be a whole lot better
if he had sex once a day
on weekdays and twicet on Saturdays
when she came out of the office
he asked her what the Dr. said
with everybody listening
she said Dr. Tubbs said
you're going to die
on the next visit
Dr. Tubbs told Hooter
he had to get serious with her
said We can operate on him
try to get it out but you need to know
that would probley make him
pure flat impotent
she said Well that's fine
but would there be
any negative side effects?
that piece of gossip
brought her right back
to her previous hero status

5

he ran off home to Arkansas
where we heard he died
and the church ladies social club
decided it wasn't right
Hooter should be alone

took her out to the old Wheaton place
where her ex Paulie Joe
who it was thought
still pined for her
had put in a trailer house
over the foundation of the burned out
Wheaton Texas-house with a sitting porch
pulled up he was lounging
on the furniture outside all bigfat
with his shirt off grinning
needing a haircut
in the sunshine
she said Turn the car around
and get me out of here right now
they said What for?
he's wanting real bad
to get back together with you
she said He looks like
a Chester white hog sitting up
with two rows of titties
hanging out down his front
I don't need the reminder
or the competition

wasn't anything they could do
but take her back
she turned to look at him one last time
standing up waving his arms
his whole front belly looked like
a little boy sloshing in the bathtub
spillwaves going up and down
she said Oh set down
you silly sonofabitch
you're embarrassing me
Sybil Cockrum almost run the car

off in the ditch
them church social club women
laughed all the way in to town
they all sworn a vow
not to ever tell anybody
Ruth Lee laughed so hard
she peed herself on the carseat

6

then Maurine Huffman told
her boy Bobby Jack after that
about Hooter back in high school
how she was world famous
all the way to Abilene
put a boy in the hospital
for making fun of her
and then why
pretty soon the whole town
was all over it again
she was once more our celebrity

but when the new Campbellite
preacher's wife Sister Parker
without understanding the true essence
of the matter said
as part of her conversational duty
checking out at her register
at Piggly Wiggly I heard
somebody say you was
really something way back when
that you was maybe
the most famous person in this part of Texas
Hooter said Yes ma'am
we all were

legends in our own minds
but that was then
and today is now
and that's ezactly why
most stories start Once upon a time
and then go straight
backwards from there
but at least mine
had a point to it
and the right two words
for a conclusion
so we don't have to think
about any of it any more
and that's just about
all they are to it
I hope you have
a real nice rest of the day
and we all decided with her
it was time to let it go

Winter Solstice

A young sea breeze blown from the gulf
   Curls beneath a live oak
Nestled in the lap of twilight

Tonight's new moon released from the underworld
   Like a Frostweed blossom climbs
Into moist, dark embrace

Stars a scatter of bright colored flowers
   Gather in a joyous procession,
Jeweled Buddhas belling the heavens

A white feather of frozen cloud glowshimmers
   Like an earth-radiant halo
Glory in all its plenitude

and Another Reason

*to the Town Board while discussing
the new home-ec. teacher lecturing
her students on human reproduction*

You town fathers
are pretending to think
all the rest of us
don't remember how much
we was aware of back then
I can say for a fact
that two of you
knew I had calluses
on my nipples
by the time
I was a senior

*from the sidebar minutes of the monthly
Town Board Meetings
17 March 1960*

Ensalada

I am the sliced jalapeno
atop the spread
of red sauce
over the warm tortilla
covered with a blanket
of melted cheddar
spraddled in the center
of a brightly painted
rimchipped Mexican saucer

You are the rounds
Of pickled beet
Lightly sprinkled with
Coarse ground black pepper
A pinch of sea salt
And a small dollop
Of bleu cheese dressing
At rest within
The immaculate white bowl

for Jan, with love

Coda

After the third telling Bus Pennel said
it was not bragging
just relating the facts of the matter
about his blue tick hound
we all knew was Wheelis House's
that ran off and Bus found
then shaved his head and butt
to look like he had mange
with only one testicle
he bred on his red bone bitch
whelped nineteen pups
all of them still living
half on eyedropper feeding
by his current wife and kids
he was going to sell for fifteen dollars apiece
first come first serve
they had good bloodlines for coon

R. B. McCravey said he didn't need any
but it seemed more than a coincidence
that a one-eyed man had
a one-nutted dog he bred anyway
to anything that would stand for it
Ollie McDougald said it was a shame
old Bus never made a permanent hook-up
with Hooter Hagins they could of
had them together a Missing One Club
and a matching dog to show for it
Cephas Bilberry said You could
invite Wheelis House over

he could set on the porch
with his artificial leg in his lap
be a yard ornament
and bawl for the crowds going by
which we all had a good laugh on

except Bus finally said
It wadn't my fault any of that didn't happen
I axed her a dozen times
to marry me she said no
even when I had her so drunk oncet
I thought she'd agree to anything
and I offered to take her
up to Dallas or Abilene to do it
and another time when we both
was still married to somebody else
neither one of us didn't like no more
she wouldn't have any part of it
no matter how hard I tried
And that's sorta a funny thing
said Clovis Ledbitter yall were
always real close growing up
I for one would have bet all the money
you owe me for the last ten years
yall'd find a way to do it
still wonder about it why

Well said Bus she said that
was half the reason when I axed her
to tell me oncet and for all why not
she said that being married
wasn't any more than celibacy
all it was cracked up to be
it wasn't worth the risk
of breaking up a good friendship for

when we could get drunk together
and have a poke anytime we wanted to
Ollie McDougald said What was it
the other half of the reason then?
Bus said It was about my eye
she was afraid she'd have to be worried
any of her good friends
at the Ladies Church Social Club
might notice her husband only
had one and how she'd be embarrassed
to have them talking about her
being married to somebody
with such a malfigurement of omission
she'd never be able to hold her head up
when she walked down the street in town
that's all they are to it
and there wasn't one thing
I could think of to say back to her
that book was closed shut

Another Reason

to Joe Bob Trammel who Kristine genuinely
did not like, on general principles
which she was very sure he did not have

You are like a tomato worm
or a hemorrhoid
your only purpose on earth
is to make my character stronger

from the sidebar minutes of the monthly
Town Board Meetings
27 October 1960

Tough
Buena Vista Ragsdale

the dew lay all night heavy upon my branch
Job 29: 19

The morning the mailman found her
after eighteen hours on that caliche ground
hard as a mule trail, the dregs
of dawnlight streamed up like a cockscomb
above their rickety farmhouse ridgepole
and wallowed with the blue tick heeler
the raindrip groundedge under the Texas porch
far sky still dark blue as a shotgun barrel

above where she lay in the body length embrace
of death, wash hung stretched out and starched
on the clothesline like a flock of angels
nesting in rows under a fading daylight moon
the cheatgrass whitewashed with hard rime

she fell and then waited for him to find her
through the afternoon and cold night with
a broken hip, her dispeptic husband inside
with the T.V. wondering where supper might be
until he found buttermilk and cornbread
in the cold box with a quarter of onion
that would have to tide him over
until she finished whatever she was doing
and made him something for breakfast
never noticing she didn't come to bed

when the mailman knocked him up
from his Captain Kangaroo reverie to wallow
out of his chair and come answer the door
he said You need to get on the phone
call an ambulance to come out here
he said What for? I aint sick yet
the mailman said It's not about you
it's your wife Miss Buena laying out there
on the ground half froze to death and hurt bad
it looks like and he said
I wondered how come she hadn't made no coffee

she wouldn't even take an aspirin
with a glass of whiskey for the pain
so she could stay awake and keep her mind
alert enough to hear what that dammed Dr. Tubbs
and those nurses might be saying
about her behind her back
who didn't know a sonofabitching thing
about it anyway and after
the mailman offered his opinion
on how tough she was she said
Like a ocotillo limb to which Dr. Tubbs
said What? She said A devil's walking stick
just find a bed and put me in it
I need to get some rest

her husband hitched a ride in
with the mailman the next day and sat
in a corner of her room saying nothing,
like a waterlogged raft waiting
for a huge shove to get underweigh
but accepting a dinner tray when they brought it
then hitched a ride back to the farm

every evening with whoever he conned
out of a lift the seven miles
so introverted and evanescent
the nurses and Dr. Tubbs on rounds
never even noticed his presence
he made such a science of mute insociability
except to ask that the channel be changed
on rare occasions of documentary or political commentary
beyond his cognition, having as Dr. Tubbs said
the mental capacity and vocabulary
of a second grader plus the word firetruck

she lay dying through the winter
with her nonhealing shattered pelvis and femur
uncomplaining and acceptant of fate
only asking the nurses one request,
that the call switch be hung
on the toilet paper holder saying
By god they can find me being dead
in bed or on the ground but
they are not going to discover me
stretched out on top of the bed pan
when her husband said What
was that about? She said
Just shut up, your mind is as black
as a table of face down dominoes
on top of a midnight velvet cloth
go on home you aint doing anybody any good
so you might as well do it there as here

Dr. Tubbs said she was a lily of the field
her toiling and spinning days done
let her have anything she wants
anybody who put up with that man

and that hard a life out there alone
for fifty years is a candidate for sainthood

not to speak also of the fact she could do
any job needed to be done on a ranch or farm
from building fence to pulling calves
to digging a new outhouse pit and moving the shack on
to fixing gates, swathing and pitching hay to picking up eggs
mailman said he'd seen them going out to work
she carrying tools in a shoulder satchel
he following like something habitual
carrying an empty five gallon bucket
he'd turn down and sit on
while she worked, all the time fulfilling
his self-designated role supervising and criticizing
once when he brought the mail out he saw her
pushing a lawnmower over the front yard weeds
her life object telling her where she had to go back
for a missed spot she said Get out of the way
go back in the house or I'll mow your feet

no one in town had a goose's idea
where she found him, how she taught
him to walk unless she bought him
a peep of chickens to be examples
or got him toilet trained, he in our minds
the veritable emblem of the reason
we invented the concept of uselessness
thank God he married a woman who knew
how a deep well bucket pulley system worked or he
would have died of thirst staring at the sink
his presence no longer a matter
she had time or energy to think about
it being nothing worth the effort

in March after almost one hundred and eighty days abed
she asked the young R.N. just out
of Temple Nursing School if she would find someone
to go out to her house and look in her closet
bring her white longdress
up to the hospital if it wouldn't be trouble
when the nurse who had not yet been told
arguing with Miss Buena Vista
was like arguing with an axe
asked Why'd you need it for?
she only looked at her with her owlstare
until she said Yes ma'am I will find somebody
to do that even if I have to do it myself
she said I would be much obliged
would you have them hang it up
in the wardrobe side by my bed?

the head night nurse said She would
have looked a banshee eye to eye
through the hospital window where she laid
for all those months and told him
in front of company or Dr. Tubbs
Get the hell out of here you sonofabitch
and if he had any sense, by God he would

on an equinox day when the sunrise and moonset
painted both corners of her long window at dawn
a nurse walking by heard her say Okay
I'm done with it, get out of the way
I'm coming through
by the time she got in she was already gone
her hair combed, wearing her white dress
no one could imagine how she got out
of the wardrobe closet and on her body

with her spiral broken hip
hands folded together pretty

they called Dr. Tubbs who came
and felt her pulse said like a mortician
She has expired and started writing
on the chart to make it official
when her husband stood and held up his hands
like he was exposing a stigmata
asked Is she dead then?
everybody shocked because they had
once again forgotten his presence in the room
and her eyes came open looking right at him
she said You can go home Ralph
Go home now Now
and she closed her eyes and was dead again

Dr. Tubbs said I believe Miss Buena
would agree with me when I say
I'll be goddammed, and no one said No she wouldn't
the nurse said I've never seen that before
Ralph said I'll be going home now
I believe she gone off and left me for good
Dr. Tubbs said I believe Miss Buena
would tell me to go to hell if she heard me say
O God I loved that woman
I would have kept her as my patient
every day of my life

but Miss Buena I want you to know
if you can hear me, just in the unlikely event
there is indeed an afterlife,
I sincerely hope we are in separate chambers
with my luck there will be a pet rattlesnake

in your room and when it finally strikes you
St. Peter will come running for me
to come in and check on that poor snake
heal it up and all forgive it for what it in ignorance did
and I suspect on my last day on earth
that memory will cover me like a cast iron potlid

What Billy Klogphorne Said
To His Son Willy John After His Twelfth Birthday

Your mama told me
to have a man to man
talk with you, son,
about the birds and the bees

I know you understand the theory
of mammalian reproduction
you've grown up on a gentleman's farm

what I want to tell you
is the sum of wisdom
I have accumulated after half a life
being joined to one woman

there are two things, Willy John,
a married woman will avoid
anytime it is possible

I can get them both
welded into the same sentence
not in any special order
They have no love for sex or football

that's my advice to you if you want it
on how to plan out the last
fifty or sixty years of your life

and as far as I know that's pretty much
what there is to it

Amanda Strayhorn, Reverend's Wife
or
Sex with the Apostle Paul by Braile
A Tale of Paradise Lost in Once Upon a Time Texas

Till I come, give attention to reading,
to exhortation, to doctrine
11 Timothy 4:13

Strophe

Whilom he was Reverend Strayhan for years
then somewhere around exactly the time of the disobedience
and divorce it started the great shift to Strayhorn
which took approximately three years more or less
to become the final authorized version when even
the bank, Post Office, Ministerial Alliance, his congregation
and the football booster's club recognized it as official

it was his wife and then ex-wife
who invented it under the artificial name authors use
the secret emerging in strategic literary gatherings
and from those libidinous tales she penned
that she thought no one would ever read
until they came forth like Lazarus in the women's magazines
and she became famous and finally exceedingly rich

according to her telling of the saga as Amanda Strayhorn
they were a typical unhappily married couple
with five obstreperous children whose birthdays
were as much a mystery to the Reverend
as Greek, dishwashing or putting the toilet lid down
he did the preaching, zeal maintenance and overlording
she worked on being pregnant and subservient

the great breakthrough in his life she said
was his accidental but inspired discovery of Coors beer
as he had always endured powerful cravings for libation
which being a Reverend provided adequate excuse
for guilt and shame to whet character upon
but when he found a brew with no taste whatsoever
he interpreted it as a sign from God

as tastelessness for him deduced impossibility of sin
which could only be driven by carnal appetite
therefore he might imbibe with the same pleasure
he took in reading dreary scriptures of the Apostle Paul
as author she said when he came to that divinely inspired
understanding he was happy as a puppy who discovered
he had two peters hooked up to two separate drive systems

which liberated him to the rational understanding of
his mentor hero Paul's credo that all things are possible
to those who love the Lord which for him
created a brave new world of possibility through limitation
meaning initially he could eat or drink anything and all of
    it he desired
if he only gave up adding cayenne pepper, bitters, lime peel
or anchovies whose deprival gave him exceeding joy

soon the pangs of hedonism were shunted forever
as the depth of his study to show himself approved
unto his Lord, rightly dividing his own words of truth
lead him to a pathway of self-justification through
sensual sacrifice which allowed him to enjoin
himself deprived unto the pleasures of the flesh
in order to exalt himself through witness and testimony

which eventually pointed directly to their bedroom
when it was revealed unto him he no longer
need fear shame regarding his hidden love
for the female shape hip joint thigh and breast
but that he could express his inner needs
through suppression of the primary entrance of sight
requiring external illumination to be extinguished

prior to entrance within the garden of bliss which
to his interpretation meant since he was almost blind
he could take off his glasses before engaging
the bedroom and proceed to enjoy the wonders
of conjugal delight through deprivation of sight
which would intensify the inner light of spiritual union
and thereby expand his prowess to the Lord's great approval

all of which he worked out with diligent prayers unceasing
in a manner which he convinced himself pleasing unto God
as it allowed him to celebrate the scriptural Sabbath
by finishing the last touches on his Sunday sermon
and spend the rest of the afternoon joyfully emparadised
with his lovely mate, yielding with coy submission and sweet
amorous delay as they cleaved one unto another

which Amanda Strayhorn the authoress described
as requiring her to patiently await the entrance
of her Lord and Master into Eden's bridal bower
every Saturday afternoon after he worked himself
into an erotic frenzy writing sermons on Satanic temptation
of Baptist youth into the fires of hell through visions
of sexual degradation upon which he expounded with vigor

whereupon he would come to the bedroom
naked as Adam and half blind with a leading anticipation
that made him appear as if he were riding a unicorn
fling open the door and shout Behold
thy lord cometh to thee to make great pleasure
and ready or not he was upon her like an octopus
sticking carrots into a bowl of kneaded bread dough

this activity continuing so many seasons that
she came to understand finally the full meaning
of the concept of eternity including assets and liabilities
but lead to an alternate knowledge of creativity
inspired by the Reverend's use of scripture
and hymn after his entrance salutation often
bursting into "I come to the garden alone"

or "To the work to the work we are children of God"
or the self-addressed "Stand up stand up for Jesus" and then
when he oft entered her ungently as a result
of his personally invoked and rapacious mental constructions
he initiated movement by way of sacred reference
"Shadrach Meshach and In-we-go" or
"Count thy many blessings: one two three four five six seven....

so that she learned to counter the reverence
of his efforts stroke by stroke, tit for tat,
joint by joint, urge by urge through song and text
softly singing "for there's no other way to be happy
in Jesus but to trust and obey" and at the mark of final
    consummation
whispering "When he shall come he shall be glorified
and admired by all   Second Thessalonians 1:10"

and in the words of the short story writer Amanda Strayhorn
that Muse encouragement into her still small voice
flowed through his ear into his throbbing brain
and blew his entire tiny mind down, out, and through him
to the point that she became an inspired scriptural prodigy
whispering Malachi 3:1 starting softly, then rising,
building like a small earthquake

or when on rare occasions he would enter shyly
as if he had engendered second thought misgivings over
his private sacred personal theological credo
she would offer encouragement with Mark 1:7
thus he would not gorge the remainder of the day
with pouting, sorrow and pity for himself Amanda said
that power was almost enough to persuade her

to become a Strayhorn Felix Agrippa Christian
then on a rainy day she could be appropriate with
Revelation 1:7 or when members of the flock were scheduled
for supper that evening she quoted Jude 14
and once when he pondered aloud in wonderment over what
his congregation thought about their personal and private lives
had anybody ever said anything about that to her?

she held his perspiring head between her hands and
smilingly recited third John three and he waxed pleased
enjoying so much as a personal favorite
her initiating their Sabbath ritual with Titus 3:12
and then on a day when he was laboring over
a proper ending for his holy performance she whispered
"Do thy diligence to come before winter Second Timothy 4: 21"

Antistrophe

At the divorce hearing after questioning
she had to admit finally and in truth, yes, she was in fact
Amanda Strayhorn, having been inspired to choose that
appellation because Amanda was his mother's name
which seemed appropriate and Strayhorn
because the image of a horn as on a charging rhinoceros
was her best description of his Sabbath behavioral mode

it took many prior seasons for our town ponderance
whether the famous Amanda Strayhorn author
in the women's magazines at the beauty shop
might be somehow some way our little Alice
since no one could imagine her in that personal light
so worn out after deliverance of five children in immediate order
before Dr Tubbs, as we suspected, took issue

bringing enough to browbeaten enough
in her proper Christian subservient role
perched on the left end second row from the front
every Sunday with her six pound Bible
lapped in the shadow of one of the seven enormous hats
she churched faithful to Paul's First Corinthians 11:5 et al.
    admonition
the veritable epitome of perfect reverential helpmeet

Lilly McCree our high school librarian
and designated arbiter of literary jurisprudence
being first to point out resilient affinity
between character, author, and potential community prodigy
to which LaVon Fleming said What did she say?
and Delfinia Martin the beautician washing her hair said
I think she thinks she's simulur to somebody we known

thus sprach Zarathustra and in the space
of a subaltern deity's heartbeat the rumor flamed
like a homecoming bonfire before the Tahoka game
and spread like the great dustcloud harbingering Texas
spring cotton planting until the heretofore meek and mild
Alice Strayhan might as well have personally and in entirety
   like Moses
parted the Red Sea and drowned Tahoka's football coaching staff

to the point that every woman in Garza County
took on the diligent role of literary scholar
scouring shelves and archives of libraries
over the known world all the way to Lubbock
searching for every word penned by or ascribed to
the great authoress Amanda Strayhorn
upturning the applecart mores of our community

in their zeal to endeavor and persevere
toward ascertainment of the true and final identity
of the object of their seething potential adoration
without once ever asking the Reverend's wife
whether she knew one thing about it or not
to the point that when a new Amanda Strayhorn
romantic tale was published, no copy of that woman's magazine

could be found within one hundred miles
of our town so that one day that life-changing spring
when a new story appeared in print, a gathering of the coven
took place at Brenda's Curl Up and Dye Hair House
and Lilly McCree who first received the magazine
at the high school library and promptly hid it away
in order to uphold the morals of our youth

upon questioning declared the tale salacious
to which LaVon Fleming rejoined What does that mean?
upon which Matty Evelyn Collier said It probably means
it was one she read four times before
she went to bed that night to which
Mozell Williams said Oh no where is it now?
Lilly McCree beneath the dryer smiled and said Six actually

the maelstrom of the rumor mill eventually churned
its way to the veritable foundations of Texas society
reaching the portals of the First Baptist Church itself
flotsam and jetsam washing over hardwood floors
up to the very Reverend's study door where he
as innocent and ignorant as the non-existent
Texas snow our parents walked four miles uphill through

on their way to school all the days of their youths
awaited the seminal moment of enlightenment
destined to change his life and identity forever
which he in a perfectly reverential and pastoral manner
deflected in the time honored Protestant tradition
of indifference and denial, knowing in his heart
nothing of the such could happen under his watch

Epode

the hamartia finally revealed, inscribed and then expunged
by the catharsis of the episode of the size seven red shoes
given to Billy Lou Hill in patent leather to wear
to the Junior-Senior Prom she was not allowed to attend
as dancing was to be tolerated, that being an abomination
before the Lord, the veritable emblem of Mark 3:29 and
    Matthew 12:31
the Unforgiven Sin clearly and irrevocably established

by Wade Guy, a Catholic, thereby double damned
before the eyes of her Christian parents Bill and Billy Hill
the entire affair thrown on the trash heap of abeyance
that potential relationship being declared null and void
until the two got in his pick-up and drove to Via Acuna, Mexico
where they got hitched in that heart of darkness
much to the chagrin and Horror of both sets of parents

Bill Hill pere and Billy Hill mare gathering
Billy Lou Hill's clothing into a suitcase and carting it
to the Baptist churchhouse to be given to widows and orphans
and sick and afflicted until they changed their collective mind
went back and brought it home in the event
Billy Lou grew up and came to her senses or they discovered
they actually sort of liked Wade Guy, except for the red shoes

which Alice Strayhan found while cleaning
the First Baptist Church storeroom one Saturday morning
while fasting and praying in preparation for the Sabbath ritual
those same slippers sliding like Cinderella's upon her feet
to which her heart lept up in size seven jubilation
and which she carried under her arm to the bedroom
to be put away privily like Mary's unborn baby

then hail muse et cetera when the Lord of the Manor
appeared as though through a veil darkly
that afternoon entering the Garden of Paradise
to assume his role as head of his household
as Christ Jesus is the head of His true church
taking that which was rightfully his as husband
the wife leaving her parents and cleaving unto him

in the midst of their emparadised throes
Alice Strayhan at The critical juncture of her life
whilst he strove mightily laboring in the field of the Lord
lifted her legs upward before her sight both
and breathed a great sigh upon which he,
greatly move'd like the Prince of the Capulets and Montagues,
turned his hubris and great neck and above him saw

red shoes suspended within the ether upon which
he as in William Tell's Overture leaped from the saddle
grasped his wife's pure as the driven snow ankle
and screamed Galatians and Ephesians!
upon which he saw above him floating sheaves
as if he were Ezekiel entering the state of holy vision
leapt to his feet, secured and put on his spectacles

before him in gay profusion and taped
to the ceiling dozens of dove wing white paper sheets
filled with scriptural verses pertinent
to their private moments of conjoined rapture

and then betwixt and centered: the typewritten proof corrected
    draft
of a new short story chronicling the sabbatical endeavors
of one Amanda Strayhorn, Reverend's Wife

Whore he screamed holding the shining patent leather slipper
he had torn from her foot Red Whore of Babylon
Concubine of Satan you Harlot you Lillith you Jezebel
you evil evil Evil Sinner before God, the Apostle Paul and man
I renounce you before Heaven's portal, I renounce you
before All that is ... and she whispered in a still, small voice
Would you and the Apostle Paul shut the fuck up?

and he astounded fell into a great swoon and lay aback
stricken by a great thunderbolt wrapped in a mighty wind
and she rolled away from him like the great gravestone of Christ
reached forth her hand and jerked away her patent leather
size seven red shoe from his great feigned dying grasp
placed it upon her foot to her great pleasure
and in naked majesty walked out of his life forever

The trial came and went like the seasons of time
some say the high water mark in our town's recorded history
whereupon she revealed her alter ego and identity
and upon final dissolution of marital status
took upon herself permanently her created name and identity
little knowing that even then she would be linked
by pseudonym to the object of her contempt forever

time moved on and so did we
she left us in flesh, we kept her in spirit
the Ladies Literary Society even taking the name
Amanda Strayhorn Memorial Women's Book Group
Whilom the ex-husband toiled on, to our great astonishment

maintaining his ministerial position, waxing dignified
    eloquent zeal
Reverend Strayhorn, our personal Rhinoceros guard upon
    the Lord's steppes

For Eleanor Wilner, with love

An Elegiac Point of Honor

After it was over and done
the dust settled and nobody killed
nobody arrested and thrown in jail
people from every corner of town
said it was the best thing
that man ever did in his life
but why the hell did he quit so soon?

Ralph Ragsdale played snooker alone
because nobody wanted to shoot with him
being so inept he'd take an hour
to play and lose against himself
and also because on his best day
he was deemed a useless dullard and anybody
playing with him would be tainted by association

but on that moment he whirled and hit Odus Millard
his veritable mal-equal who every day sat by himself
on the raised wall bench hateful and miserable
contemplating conversion to Republican
with his pool cue and when he squealed
like a shoat being castrated hit him again
until he ceased squealing and then he stopped

not one person in Billy's Pool Parlour raised a hand
to break it off or hollered Yall quit it now
or called Sheriff Red Floyd
to come see if Odus was alive
or Victor Hudman at the mortuary to collect the remains
all glorying in Odus Millard's misfortune
which was universally adjudicated appropriate

after he lay whimpering
under the snooker table a sufficient time
to realize he would unfortunately survive
Bus Pennel called his wife
at the Waybourne Pig Cafe to tell her
she ought to come down and get him
if she managed a break working coffee counter

by the time she came Odus
was back sitting on the raised wall bench
wiping his face and hair
with a chalkboard erasing towel
she said Who did it?
he said That goddam Ralph Ragsdale
he hurt me real good this time

and here where they were both who swilled
at the trough of the Goddess of Second Chances
she went over to Ralph playing snooker
by himself again said Did you hit Odus
with a pool cue? And when he said Yes I did
she said How come you to stop so quick?
and he said Guess I got tored

she said You want to tell me why for?
he said Your goddammed Odus he said
the only reason Buena Vista had legs was so she
wouldn't leave a trail like a slug when she walked
she said Odus said that? About Miss Buena?
he said Yes the sonofabitch did you'gn axe him
but Odus guilty would not look up from the floor

she said Then I don't blame you and Ralph said
I don't either I heard that story before
it's about nuns, Buena Vista she wasn't
no goddam Catholic we was Baptists
and I won't have Odus Millard slurrying
her memory by the connection in this town
somebody is got to stand up for Christian womern

and she said Yes I see
and she pulled Odus off the raised wall bench
and she spitwiped the dryblood and snot tears from his face
and she got both of them in her Chevrolet pickup and she drove
Odus Millard across town to their house, walked him in and shut
    the door
and Ralph Ragsdale a hero now in the place he called home
played out his snooker game in Bill's Pool Parlour all alone

What Kristine Thornton Said
To Mayor Howard Topham in Piggly Wiggly
On a Tuesday Double S & H Green Stamp Day

March 1961

Hey you
you know anything about
what to do with constipation?

Naw
whyn't you ask Larry Joe?

He knows about a remedy?

Anybody that full of shit
oughter have some ideas
about what to do with it.

Ducktail

His fair large Front and Eye sublime declared
Absolute rule: and Hyancinthine Locks
Round from his parted forelock manly hung
Clust'ring, but not beneath his shoulders broad
                                    —PARADISE LOST, IV, 300-303

Delicious windfall apple of her father's eye sparkling
like a newmint Rockefeller dime at her shrimp and French fry
fourteenth birthday supper raised the hair on her papa's neck
during the ceremonial lighting of the candles when she asked
Daddy, could I have a special favor for my birthday?

and Meredith blowing candles fro and asunder
said Just so you won't have to wonder, it's not about a car
Daddy that's almost the fartharest thing from my mind
why I haven't even started Driver Training Class yet
what in the world would I want a car for?

he astonished sat hard upon his chair
said aloud and with emphasis Well
and his sun rise and set offspring rejoined
Daddy, I want you to grow your hair out for me
that's what I want

let your hair grow until I say that's enough
and I promise I'll take care of it so the whole family
will be proud and get me ready for Odessa Beauty College
after I've grown up and graduated from high school
the very only thing I want for my birthday

upon which her daddy firmly interjected Well again
and he meant it sincerely
proud of his little girl as only a father can be

———

through August and up to the opening of football season
his hair grew steadily in scattered bunches
intermittent like the year's unrained upon cotton crop
careless weeds arising hither and various
only to be chopped, cultivated and manicured
by Sweet Meredith's beneficent hands

until one day as if by astonishment a luxurious mane
rested as a velvet drape upon his head in dark waves and ripples
a profusion which she tended unceasingly with slatherings
of Wildroot Cream Oil and dabs of Brylcreem
so the coiffure glistened like an ebony crown welded to his pate
carefully scissored so that nary a hair strayed from its chosen
    place

———

a Wednesday night Baptist prayer meeting
before the Friday night game with Tahoka
Phil Bob Bouchier came to him bearing hamartia
as a representative of the Pastors and Deacons Inner Council
at the behest of Reverend Strayhorn and said
It's about your hair
What about it? he said

and the Reverend Strayhorn lurking in abeyance
awaiting opportunity to excel in a profundance of homiletic
     rapture
seized upon the occasion to perform a recital of scripture as if
extracted spontaneously from deep memory quoting first Timothy
and then the shame of First Corinthians eleven verse fourteen
verbatim in an admonishment to motivate hisself up
to Lenton Ingram's barber shop and get him a haircut

so that he rosy humiliated screwed his courage to the penultimate
sticking point and told the Deacon and Reverend his goddam hair
did not go over his collar yet and it was none of their business
he'd grow it down to his ass if that's what he felt like
and with his daughter haughty on one arm and on the other
his wife walked out of prayer meeting and simultaneously
trundled them the hell out of his life

⤙ ⬦ ⤚

November Sunday after the Antelope Homecoming Game with Slaton
lost by fourteen points Meredith performed her masterpiece
with pomade and a copious waft of Aqua Net spray so that his hair
moulded into a flowing rambunctious, bouffant and truly astonishing
Elvis Presley ducktail worthy of Little Richard and the Everly Brothers
lustrous in its piled glow to invoke covetousness of the English Queen
when he walked down the 1st Presbyterian Church aisle his family atow

in exercise of his newfound religious freedom and sat himself
and his entourage in a downfront lefthand side pew hoping nobody
really noticed if he was there or not shimmering in the churchlight
until Maxine Durrant rose from her middle center bench, eased down
the aisle to the space behind him where she leaned avast and whispered
If you wore your hair like that in high school I would have screwed you
on first date, went back and seated herself in her accustomed place

he so amazed and exalted his body in confused joyous pandemonium
lept so that he had to withdraw a songbook from the rack before him
and lay it across his lap, Meredith's mother holding his hand
like Eve virtuous in the garden whispered What was that she said?
and he in response I believe she greeted us to her churchhouse
and his Mrs in joy turned in place to nod, say hidy and more
but Maxine like Lilith head-down pondered the significance of floor

twice during the sermon he like Epimetheus peered over his shoulder
Maxine Durrant-Helen of yore embraced his eye, the first time smiling
and on the second demurring gently, nodded so that before benediction
when the congregation was asked to stand before the Lord in prayer
as he began to rise the songbook fell away like a great gravestone so that
he aghast sat back down apace and then reclining to the kneeling port
adjusted his britches to a more downward position easing his discomfort

⤛✦⤜

at the Sunday meal after grace Meredith smiled
deliciously over the plate when he passed her
the pear and green pea with mayonnaise salad
and he seized the opportunity to proclaim
he was desirous to open a family conversation

and he said Well then Baby Girl
(Meredith aglow in innocence and modesty)
You said I couldn't cut my hair until we talked about it
and then after talking you agreed I could so when
can we have that talk about exactly that?

and Meredith truly a diamond resplendent
in youthful majesty opined Why Daddy
I was just going to ask you when we could speak a bit
about me getting a car now that I've passed
Driver Training Class and got my Learner's Permit

which one do you think we ought to start with first?
I have my scissors on top of my Gideon Bible you gave me
for my thirteenth birthday right in my bedroom drawer
and her gentle, loving smile filled the room with warmth and light
as if she were a candle aglow upon the dinnertable shiny and bright

And Another Reason

*to Mack Wood, Kristine's former high school boyfriend
proposing opening soil bank land to cattle grazing*

You're proof there's no such thing
as a circumcised cowboy
or one with a brain
you wouldn't have no place
to put your chew every week
when your latest squeeze reminded you
to brush your teeth

*From sidebar minutes of the monthly
Town Board Meetings
14 December 1961*

Overheard Conversation between Clovis Ledbitter and Billy Klogphorne dealing with Klogphorne's Father-to-son talk with his son Willy John

I told Robbie Van Wagoner
what you told your boy
and he said it wasn't always true
his wife likes football

Saturday Night Storm
and Amanda's Puppy is Frightened

(after Bobby Joe just called in from Junction
60 miles out on the last leg of a week-long haul)

The gods in the upper room
just flat racaucous tonight:
knocked a PBR off the counter
canclang on the bar rail, roll against the stool legs
beer seeps through the floorboards
thunder spreads across the rafters
ceiling bouncing as they dance
to the holy jukebox stormy weather pick hits
poolball clack and waft of Bull Durham and joy weed
floating through the live oaks
living high while daddy's out on ran business
or wallowed up against chthonic big legged mama

the warm libation drips and drips
all across the hill country
and the dog shivers against the night sounds
screaming witches and caterwauls
singing loud enough to peel wallpaper
Jupiter and Saturn torn away
from the milky way and moon
on the kid's bedroom walls
all the lunges the lightning
shoves into the warm sky
begs me to let him up in our bed
but he's pure shit out of luck

Go away baby dog
you're on your own this time
it's a storm a raging all both
out there and in here tonight
fast and pray however you do it
doggy style, work out your own
salvation with fear and trembling
your new daddy will be home in an hour
I'm planning to tie a double knot
up in my own redemption righteously tight
I'm singing Come come ye saints
nookie's on the agenda this rainy night

Three Items in Our Fridge
Awaiting My Husband
In Bandera, Tejas
60 Miles Distant

A quart of pickled okra

Eight cans of Lone Star Beer

One large, unopened bottle
of astonishing Jose Cuervo
1800 Reposado
perfectly aged
and desperately lonely

Another Reason

If I'm commanded to love my neighbor
Larry Joe
I'm glad as hell
You live on the other side of town

From the sidebar minutes of the monthly
Town Board Meeting
January 1962

Song E.U. Washburn the Gravetender Heard
While Tending Roses Over the Grave
Of Philemon and Baucis Rojas
1 Corinthians 13:13

Amor, ch'a nullo amato amar perdona,
Mi prese del costui piacer si forte,
Che, come vedi, ancor non m'abbandona.
—Dante, *INFERNO*, V, 103-105

Is it true that Love is God? she asked.
And he said, Yes, oh yes, it is true, my love,
but you must remember
to try and never believe it that way.

And then do you believe? she asked.
And he said, Yes, I believe beyond death
in believing, yes.
That faith one can never fully give up,
there will always be doubt.

You must also remember to hope
and that in our language to wait
and to hope are one.
Espera, querida, espera.

And then what should I hope for? she asked.
And he said, With all your heart
you must hope
that Love will keep believing in you.
Have faith in that alone

for only then will the world
as we believe in it continue
and that is God
and that is enough.

Overheard at Adolph's coffee counter One Morning
By Harold Rushing and Dan Cockrum:
Joe Bob Trammel Blowing Off Steam
After Town Board Meeting

By god
if I could
I'd write a book
about Kristine Thornton
one day

on the other hand
that might
be one
the world
could do without

Postmortem
After the Obsequies

1

What I remember of the past first
is a day during those days
when I wanted to sing opera,
a day when everything happened
that I cared to be inside the happening thereof:
rain crushed through the live oaks
in a wild sprint, then circled
into the meadow like a band of Comanche warriors
flashing bows and spears, come in bright warpaint
to carry me away to join Cynthia Ann Parker,
the sky filled with attack screams
and distant drum roar,
just as quickly the meadow empty
and quiet, storm moving
away like a stampeded remuda,
the world all bright color
and me right in the middle
living my life inside a rainbow

Then a three quarter waxing moon, half risen,
wallowed in the tank with a modicum of enthusiasm
and emphasis, like the teenage girl I was,
alone, shy, and waiting for no one
under the fall of perpetual nightjars
Lords of the Dance
carving traces in the sky
with their joyous roar in the feathered twilight

and into that memory traipsed
Charles E. Carr, Jr. the Second, who was my first
and only suitor to whom
I was conquest and chattel,
the fact of which I was reminded
weekly and at times daily,
not to mention his boast
thrown to anyone who cared to listen
that he won me in a Gin Rummage game,
a man who had the commanding presence
to fill any room he entered
like the effluvial waft
of digested butter beans
telling me, "bull bats, Merlean,
insignificant night birds
that never even learnt to sing,
that's what this is all about. Bull bats.
Seen one, seen 'em all."
And, with the end of magic in my life,
I became his wife.

2

It wasn't all that long after the wedding almost nobody
came to when I remember the air that one morning, still,
like it was holding down something dying to let it finish its
work, and if I made any movement, even turning my eyes
just a little to see if anything around me was alive or even
breathing, I could feel little pocketswells of cold like cur-
rent spots swimming in a lake skybolted above the earth,
but standing perfectly still I was in a hole in the universe
with nothing moving, only the suspicion of death walking
an invisible circle around me, then the hardest thunders-
mash I've ever known lifted and pitched me against the

ground. I couldn't breathe but still I tasted what seemed the color of green and my blouse stuck to my flesh like my grandmother's jalapeno jelly, melted chili pepper rivulets down my back and I remember thinking that's where my wing sockets could have been and now they're cauterized. My hair tingled like I'd just shampooed with yucca root and wild mint and it stood up with gooseflesh shivers that washed over me as if I'd fallen into a deepwater well. When I looked up, all the laundry on the clothesline had little halos on them and I laughed out loud, glad Charles hadn't put any of his underwear in the basket that week because he would have seen it as a personal miracle. That was when I heard the music, the whole sky singing and throbbing and all the trees with all the bright colors I could ever imagine dancing their sparkling leaves to the rhythm and I knew somehow right then before I had any time to think about it I was the only one who could hear it. And there he was standing right beside me and the first words he said were, "Where you been, Merlean? I was walking all over and couldn't find where you was at. Didn't you hear that lightning? You shouldn't be laying on the ground like that when it's looking like storm, you could get struck dead and rained on. You better get on up now and come in the house and think about fixing some dinner." And I saw a daylight moon right above me pulling apart the thickets of clouds so it could look down and see something it was hunting for, almost like it was searching out the earth's tide pull-trigger and I knew I was re-alive and that I'd walked through the doors of a crypt nestled in the back of an ancient cemetery from once before a time. And the breath of musty air wrapped me up in the fragrance of a salvation I'd never dreamed of, like everything I knew and believed up to then was bound up in the rusty leather smell of a closed book on a Sunday morning that never was and I was a child again with all the world before me, and I knew there was nobody in my life I could ever tell it to until this day. And I got up and followed Charles into the house. Fifty four years ago.

3

In the spring of '54
I bottled fourteen quarts
of tornado

every time he made to leave home
he would find them
in the back of my closet
and open one

the house looked
like two three year olds
and a teething puppy went through

this one time looking
for his reading glasses

behind Piggly Wiggly's
he found a copy of last week's
T. V. Guide
wanted to see what he'd missed

I guess I made them
for his libations
the missing excitement

since he said, "It aint
no color in my life."

4

I waited outside on the sidewalk that day
he went in to Bob Collier drugstore
ordered himself a limeaid
with Roy Rogers grenadine syrup
and a straw

concentrating so on his drink he walked
into a street post a half block down
spilled Roy Rogers all over his front
stood on the sidewalk and yelled,
"Well God damn Merlean."

The closest store was Maxine Durrant's
I went straight in to the panties counter
when I looked back he was standing
staring with his ruined shirt and empty soda cup
through the glass door

I picked up a pair of bright red ones, French lace,
shook them out, held them up
turned toward the door with them over my face
counted ten, lowered
he was gone

Maxine said,
"What are you doing, Mary Lynn?"
I told, she giggled like Alisoun in "The Miller's Tale"
so long she locked the door
pulled down the shade

she went to the back
brought out each of us
a paper cup of good time

she said, "It's an occasion
for us to have a girl party."

5

He went all over town haranguing, wrangling
and bargaining like the Scotchman he was
when Charlie sent him that birthday check
because anything he bought for him
would somehow be taken as a personal offense
and had to sign the card Charles E. Carr, Junior III
so he wouldn't feel the slight to his patriarchy
that money burning a hole in his pocket
he conned Gordon Hamilton down to sixty five cents
under Bill Edwards Hardware for a silly electric razor
never even knew Gordon Hamilton called me
to bring in the sixty five cents from my personal egg money
being perhaps the only chincier man in town

so proud of his brand new Braun electric razor
he'd made such a good financial deal for
and then like some Texas deus ex machina
whatever god looking down with a sardonic sense of humor
that day smote him with a case of shingles
there wasn't anything Dr. Tubbs could do
a thing about except prescribe calamine lotion
and tell him he was forbidden to shave
until the disease had run its course

forty days and forty nights Charles E. Carr Junior the Second
sat in his chair and watched the television set
rooster crow to midnight shut down I learned to pray
to come quickly like Christ's Second Coming

until I knew every program on either one
of the two channels we got from Lubbock
he didn't even have to call from the barcalounger
when it was time for me to come in
and change from seven to eleven or vice versa
it was as ingrained in my memory as catechism
or my time of the month, the whole world
inside that house turned to black and white
Howdy Doody to Lucille Ball to Friday night fights
which I would have loved to sign him up for
against any world champion mean and available

I remember the day when I received the revelation
and understood the true meaning of the Biblical flood
how that story had not one thing to do
with the man named Noah but with his wife
who had to endure forty days and forty nights
locked up in that boat with him and all those animals
being at twenty-four seven beck and call
barn swamper, feeder and nurse mom-maid
mother-in-attendance, cook and bottle washer
with nothing more to look forward to than
getting off that damn ark after it quit raining
and start being pregnant again so that
he could fulfill his duty to replenish the earth
thank god the good Lord had changed
his mind about the subduing it part
that would have been one too many for her
and the other thing of it is, we never even
got to learn what her actual name was
I doubt Noah ever mastered the pronunciation

the whole time he sat in his chair
with that razor in his lap like it was

the Ark of the Covenant to see him through the desert
of his personal affliction and could I please
bring him another sody pop or a sandwich
or run down to Piggly Wiggly and get him some
chocolate chip cookies he had a sudden craving for?
only interrupting his meditation on injustice
and the television set to hold that razor
up to his ear and turn it on so he could listen
to another source in the world capable
of producing an immaculate meaningless whine

6

Philippians 1:21

And he said, "Bretheren,
Now is the time of mourning,
The time for weeping of tears,
But this, too, shall pass and go away
As we learn the Plan of the Lord's Great Will revealed
That yea, it cometh to pass each and every one of us will one day
Die and pass and go away and be dead and gone ..."

and I thought Holy God
Jesus Christ and the Catholic's
Holy Mary Mother of God
if that's the best he can do
the Apostle Paul hater of women notwithstanding
I could be preacher
at this church

7

Coda: Last Call

In the darkest cleft of midnight
a tiny wisp of silence cowered, concealed,
hidden by a cowl of wind

So
grief, like love,
is work
that has to be done
and
I have no clue
how or whether
to begin

I read once
I don't know when or where
or why I remember
that Rossini
said he only felt grief
twice in his life:
when his mother died
and when he was on a boat
and a roasted chicken
stuffed with truffles
fell into the water
lost and gone

I know I grieved when mama died
again when Honey my best friend dog died
once more when Charles, Jr. left

for school and I knew
he would never ever really be
my little boy again
but before God I do not know
if what I feel now is grief
or something else
I don't understand
can't name

I've never known the taste of truffles
but I've lived a life
cramful with trifles
                              like
a bowl brimful to sopping over
with a concoction whose magic ingredients
I can't remember
slipped out of my hands into the sink
a potsherd broken away, everything spilt
and I don't know which to mourn
the lost recipe
or the bowl
and because I just don't
feel like bawling or cursing
or starting over another supper
I can only stand and stare
at the suption draining away
into a whirl

Lord God
it's one of those alone
hard red wine nights
foreshadowing a bloodshot tomorrow morning sky
spiral broken moon splinters scattered
all over the floor and on the furniture, lying
like breathing, open-eyed antimacassars

daring me to come sit anywhere near
pushing me out the back door scared
into the big alone

Oh, but breathe in the waft of a ghost rain
under a waxing cat scratch moon
floating through live oak
listen to the memory of a waif cinder maid
singing *Una Volta C'era Un Re*
and beneath me
exactly between my feet
a perfect moon-scarleted primrose
glistening in the rekindling of the night

Nocturne Idyll
Ike's Grocery Store, 1962
Saturday, 9:55 p.m.

Suetta Rushing met Laveda Latham
coming out the door
said Oh I'm glad I made it in time
I have to get something for dinner
for after church
did you forget too?
Laveda said no
she only needed mushroom soup
Oh yes said Suetta
that's real good
to put over leftovers
so they'll look freshmade
And green jello said Laveda
but so she wouldn't be rude
asked Suetta what she was having
I'm getting a whole half a chicken
to put in the oven
with Arsh potatoes if they
got any left she said
and mayonnaise and walnuts
so I can make a Waldorf salad
like they do at Hemphill-Wells
for their luncheons in Lubbick
I better get in before they close
the doors and plumb shut me out

Oh said Laveda
they wouldn't leave you outside

that's what they're here for this late
Well that's just exactly right
and there's no use to talking about it
and idn't that good of them said Suetta
they're such nice neighbors
and idn't it sweet to not
have to get dressed up
to come to the store like
it was Piggly Wiggly and
idn't it a right purdy night
is all I have to say
about that subject

and they looked up
as if it was the first time
to a sky where Scorpio
held Saturn in its claw
like a jewel
dug out of the bedrock aglister
beside the ripened Cheshire cat sliver moon
the whole world awash
in wind crushed cut hay perfume
roar of cricket song
pouring down our town's streets
up the caprock, across the high plains
out over the hill country
the night beautiful and mysterious
as an old friend's ghost
moving toward shadow, waving back
from an uncovered memory

Author's Note

This book began some thirteen years ago with a single poem about my first memory of Garza county, Texas, in 1948 when I was four years old. My dad had finished his college degree and got his first job as a high school history teacher, basketball coach and schoolbus driver. We rented an abandoned farm up on the caprock above town during the height of the second dustbowl days of the llano estacado. It was a new beginning for our family, and my memory is of the dought, isolation, and heat of the August summer. I wrote the poem as a memory exercise set by Bill Kloefkorn—not to find the first memory (I can go back to the winter before my 2nd birthday in Panguitch, Utah in 1942), but to find a first moment of epiphany in my life.

Acknowledgments

The author wishes to thank the editors of the following literary magazines and journals where the poems in this book originally appeared: *Clover: A Literary Rag, Connotations, Cortland Review, Cutthroat, 15 Bytes, Hobble Creek Review, Juxta-Prose, The Missouri Review, Oregon Literary Review, Paddlefish, Poetry East, Sierra Nevada Review, Southwest American Literature, Sugar House Review, Weber: The Contemporary West,* and *Zine: Velvet Tail.*

"Piggly Wiggly," "Hooter," "Coda," and "Amanda Strayhorn, Reverend's Wife" originally appeared in *Narrative Magazine.* "Amanda Strayhorn, Reverend's Wife" was a *Narrative Magazine* Outstanding Poem of the Year.

The author wishes to thank the following Presses where some of these poems found their original incarnations or subsequent appearances: Copper Canyon Press (*Day's Work, My Town, News from Down to the Café* and *A Legacy of Shadows*), Logan House Press (*A House Made of Time*, with William Kloefkorn), Spoon River Poetry Press (*Covenants,* with William Kloefkorn), Wings Press (*Moments of Delicate Balance,* with William Kloefkorn), and Wood Works Press (*The Fish* and *Texas Wild Flowers*); as well as the following anthologies: *Red Thread, Gold Thread,* Academy of American Poets *Poem-a-Day* Series, *The Women,* and *Best of the Net Anthology.*

For patient, incredibly thoughtful, and wonderful-bordering-on-the-magnificent readings, suggestions, encouragement and critical reactions to this manuscript that went light years beyond the call of duty or friendship: mahalo, gratzi, muchas gracias, copious thanks to my three readers, Eleanor Wilner, my muse, sister, and goddess incarnate; and my amazing friends Rob Van Wagoner and Robert Behunin, who I claim as hermanos.

Special thanks to Don Esteban Nightingale, el hermano magnifico, for the loan of Sky Ranch House of Owls, where I found my way back to this book after a time of mourning.

And thanks to the following incomplete list of friends and family who encouraged me along the way: Owl and Evie, Bryce El Editor estupendo, Deanna and Mike, Cheryl, Dianne, Camille, Peg, Cookie, and the Boulder, Utah Wild Bunch, Sam Green, John Lane, Paul Hunter, Jim Brummels, Bill Kloefkorn, Kent Haruf, Justin, Amiho, Sarah, Mikel, Gailmarie, Bill and Joan, TTW, the Brucer, Rev It Up, Ken Sanders, the Servid Clan, Mary Lee Adler, Possum and the Blonde, MariaDulce, Jon and JoDee who have grown to be more kith than kin, and especially Jan, a grandmother-Beelah and fellow road warrior, who kept me on track with this book for nine years, all the way, both in the goading and caressing modes, and without whose influence this one would have never seen the light of day. And as Eleanor said, "and for all of those without whom — and that would include even the first fish that crawled out of the ooze and headed for the stars," abrazos y amor: te amo, all yall.

About the Author

David Lee was raised in West Texas, a background he has never completely escaped, despite his varied experiences as a seminary student, a boxer and semi-pro baseball player (the only white player to ever play for the Negro League Post Texas Blue Stars) known for his knuckleball, a hog farmer, and a decorated Army veteran. Along the way he earned a Ph.D., taught at various universities, and recently retired as the Chairman of the Department of Language and Literature at Southern Utah University.

Lee was named Utah's first Poet Laureate in 1997, and has received both the Mountains & Plains Booksellers Award in Poetry and the Western States Book Award in Poetry. Lee received the Utah Governor's Award for lifetime achievement in the arts and was listed among Utah's top twelve writers of all time by the Utah Endowment for the Humanities. He is the author of twenty books of poetry. In 2004, *So Quietly the Earth* was selected for the New York Public Library's annual "Books to Remember" list. His latest is *Last Call* (Wings Press, 2014). In 2014, Lee was awarded an Honorary Doctorate in Arcane Letters. He is currently in advanced training to achieve his goal of becoming a World Class Piddler.

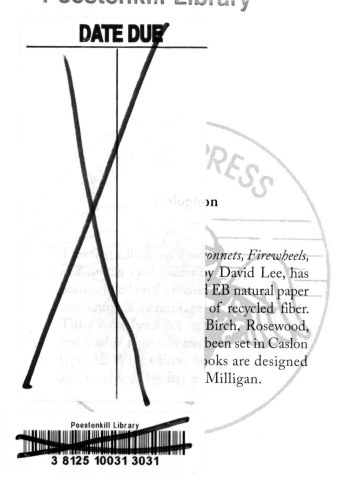

Colophon

This first edition of *Bluebonnets, Firewheels,
and Blood-eyed Sunrise*, by David Lee, has
been printed on 55 pound EB natural paper
containing a percentage of recycled fiber.
Titles have been set in Birch, Rosewood,
and Caslon type; text has been set in Caslon
type. All Wings Press books are designed
and produced by Bryce Milligan.

On-line catalogue and ordering:
www.wingspress.com

Wings Press titles are distributed
to the trade by the
Independent Publishers Group
www.ipgbook.com
and in Europe by
www.gazellebookservices.co.uk

Wings Press was founded in 1975 by Joanie Whitebird and Joseph F. Lomax, both deceased, as "an informal association of artists and cultural mythologists dedicated to the preservation of the literature of the nation of Texas." Publisher, editor and designer since 1995, Bryce Milligan is honored to carry on and expand that mission to include the finest in American writing—meaning all of the Americas, without commercial considerations clouding the choice to publish or not to publish.

Wings Press produces multicultural books, chapbooks, ebooks, CDs, and broadsides that, we hope, enlighten the human spirit and enliven the mind. Everyone ever associated with Wings has been or is a writer, and we believe that writing is a transformational art form capable of changing the world, primarily by allowing us to glimpse something of each other's souls. Good writing is innovative, insightful, open-minded and interesting. But most of all it is honest.

Likewise, Wings Press is committed to treating the planet as a partner. Thus the press uses as much recycled material as possible, from the paper on which the books are printed to the boxes in which they are shipped.

As Robert Dana wrote in *Against the Grain*, "Small press publishing is personal publishing. In essence, it's a matter of personal vision, personal taste and courage, and personal friendships." Welcome to our world.